Favourite Hymns

Continuum Icons

Great books never go out of style, but they can go out of print. The Icons series is an attractively packaged collection of the greatest works of well-known authors. Enjoy them for the first time, or take some time to reacquaint yourself with these wonderful writers.

Books in the series include:

An Intelligent Person's Guide to Catholicism   Alban McCoy

Angels Keep Their Ancient Places   Noel O'Donoghue

Angels of Grace   Anselm Grün

Anglican Difficulties   Edward Norman

Anglicanism: The Answer to Modernity   Duncan Dormor,
  Jack McDonald and Jeremy Caddick

Art and the Beauty of God   Richard Harries

C. S. Lewis: A Short Introduction   Philip Vander Elst

Favourite Hymns   Marjorie Reeves and Jenyth Worsley

God Matters   Herbert McCabe

God Still Matters   Herbert McCabe

His Love is a Fire   Brother Roger of Taizé

Lent with Evelyn Underhill   G. P. Mellick Belshaw

Letters of Direction   Abbé de Tourville

Mr Moody and the Evangelical Tradition   Timothy George

Six World Faiths   W. Owen Cole

Story of Taizé   J. L. Gonzalez Balado

The Living Gospel   Luke Timothy Johnson

Through the Year with Jesus   Anselm Grün

Tripersonal God   Gerald O'Collins

What Anglicans Believe   David L. Edwards

Women in Christianity   Hans Küng

Favourite Hymns

2000 Years of Magnificat

ꙮꙮ

Marjorie Reeves and
Jenyth Worsley

When the sun rises,
do you not see a round disk of fire,
somewhat like a Guinea? O no, no, I see an
innumerable company of the heavenly host crying
'Holy, holy, holy, is the Lord God Almighty'.

William Blake

continuum
LONDON • NEW YORK

Continuum

The Tower Building, 11 York Road, London SE1 7NX
15 East 26th Street, New York, NY 10010

www.continuumbooks.com

First published 2001

Reprinted 2003

This edition first published 2004

British Library Cataloguing-in-Publication Data
A catalogue record for this book is available from the British Library.

ISBN 0-8264-7723-2

Designed and typeset by BookEns Ltd
Printed and bound in Great Britain by
Cromwell Press Ltd, Trowbridge, Wilts

Contents

Illustrations

Acknowledgements

We wish to thank the following people for their criticisms, suggestions and research help: Madeline Barber, the Revd Dr Grayson Carter, Albert Chatterley, Anne M. Hart, Richard Jeffery, Dr Elaine Kaye, Peter McMullin, Dr Paul Ranger and Anne Ridler. We also thank our faithful typist, Jane Morgan, who has seen this book through a number of drafts.

We acknowledge with gratitude the use of the following sources on which we have chiefly drawn for information: *Abide with Me: The World of Victorian Hymns*, Ian Bradley; *The Oxford Dictionary of the Christian Church*, ed. F. E. Cross and E. A. Livingstone; *The Oxford Companion to Music* Percy Scholes, ed. John Owen Ward 10th edn; *The Oxford Companion to English Literature*, ed. Margaret Drabble; *Hymns and Human Life*, Erik Routley; *Dictionary of Christian Spirituality*, ed. Gordon Wakefield.

We thank Libby Purves for permission to quote from her *Holy Smoke: Religion and Roots. A Personal Memoir* (Hodder & Stoughton, London, 1998).

Where copyright permission has been granted for certain hymns, tunes and illustrations, we have acknowledged this on page 198. We have endeavoured to trace all material within copyright and offer apologies if any items have been missed.

Abbreviations

JC	John Cosin
PD	Percy Dearmer
WD	William Draper
JMN	John Mason Neale
FBT	F. Blair Tucker
RVW	Ralph Vaughan Williams
CW	Catherine Winkworth

OTHER ABBREVIATIONS

adapt.	adapted
arr.	arranged
C.	century
c.	circa
ed.	edited
edn	edition
et al.	and others
harm.	harmonized
ibid.	cited above
ms.	manuscript
op. cit.	in the work cited
sub nom.	under name
tr.	translated
trad.	traditional

An asterisk after a name indicates further references in the index.

List of hymns

List of hymns

St Thomas Aquinas 1227–74 tr. James Woodford	Thee we adore	Geoffrey Webber
The Coventry Carol C. 15th	Lully lulla	from Thomas Sharp's 1591 ms.
Bianco of Siena d. 1434 tr. R.F. Littledale	Come down, O love divine	Ralph Vaughan Williams 1872–1958

PART II   SIXTEENTH TO EIGHTEENTH CENTURIES

Martin Luther 1483–1546 tr. T. Carlyle	A safe stronghold our God is still	Luther, arr. J. S. Bach 1685–1750
William Kethe d. 1594	All people that on earth do dwell	Antwerp Psalter 1537
Edmund Spenser 1552–99	Most glorious Lord of life	Henry Lawes 1596–1662
Philipp Nicolai 1556–1608 tr. Burkitt	Wake, O wake!	Nicolai, harm. J. S. Bach
M. Rinkart 1586–1649 tr. CW	Now thank we all our God	J. Crüger c. 1647
George Herbert 1593–1633	King of glory, King of peace	John David Jones 1827–70
	Teach me, my God and King	Sandys Christmas Carols 1833
	Let all the world in every corner sing	Basil Harwood 1859–1949
Paul Gerhardt 1607–76 tr. RB	O Sacred head, sore wounded	trad. German melody, harm. JSB
	The duteous day now closeth	secular melody, harm. JSB
John Milton 1608–74	Let us, with a gladsome mind	Jon Antes 1740–1811
Richard Baxter 1615–91 et al.	Ye holy angels bright	John Darwell 1731–89
John Bunyan 1628–88	Who would true valour see (He who would valiant be)	trad. English melody, arr. RVW
	He that is down, need fear no fall	trad. English carol
Thomas Ken 1637–1711	Awake, my soul …	Francois Bathélémon 1741–1808
	Glory to thee, my God, this night	Thomas Tallis c. 1505–85
Joseph Addison 1672–1719	The Lord my pasture shall prepare	Henry Carey c. 1687–1743
	The spacious firmament on high	J. Sheeles 1688–1761

	When all thy mercies, O my God	F. Gore Ouseley 1825–89
Isaac Watts 1674–1748	When I survey the wondrous Cross	adapt. E Miller 1731–1807
	O God, our help in ages past	probably W. Croft 1678–1727
	Give me the wings of faith to rise	Derek Williams b. 1945
Latin C. 17th, tr. F. Pott 1832–1909	The strife is o'er, the battle done	Palestrina/W. H. Monk
From *Lyra Davidica* C. 18th	Jesus Christ is risen to-day	Lyra Davidica
Charles Wesley 1707–88	O thou who camest from above	prob. S. Wesley 1766–1837
	Come, O thou Traveller unknown	Robert King c. 1709
	Love's redeeming work is done	Herrnhut Choralbuch c. 1740
Cologne 1710, tr. Lacey *et al.*	O come, O come, Emmanuel!	French melody, adapt. T. Helmore
Thomas Olivers from Hebrew *Yigdal*	The God of Abraham praise	trad. Hebrew melody
Latin, C. 18 86 tr. Oakely *et al.*	O come, all ye faithful	probably J. F. Wade 1711–
W. Williams 1717–91 tr. P. Williams *et al.*	Guide me, O thou great Jehovah	John Hughes 1873–1932
John Newton 1725–1807	Glorious things of thee are spoken	Joseph Haydn 1732–1809
	How sweet the name of Jesus sounds	Alexander Reinagle 1799–1877
	Amazing grace!	American folk melody
William Cowper 1731–1800	O for a closer walk with God	Scottish Psalter 1635
	God moves in a mysterious way	Scottish Psalter 1635 adapt.
William Blake 1757–1827	And did those feet (*Jerusalem*)	Hubert Parry 1848–1918
Joseph Mohr 1792–1848 tr. J.F. Young	Silent Night, Holy Night	Franz Gruber 1787–1863

PART III   NINETEENTH AND TWENTIETH CENTURIES

Henry Francis Lyte 1793–1847	Abide with me	W. H. Monk 1828–89

List of hymns

John Henry Newman 1801–90	Lead, kindly Light	C. H. Purday 1799–1855/ J. B. Dykes 1823–76/ W. H. Harris 1883–1973
	Firmly I believe and truly	Warwickshire ballad, arr. RVW
	Praise to the Holiest in the height	J. B. Dykes 1823–75
Alfred Tennyson 1809–92	Strong Son of God, immortal Love	Orlando Gibbons 1583–1625
F. W. Faber 1814–63	There's a wideness in God's mercy	John Stainer 1840–63
	My God, how wonderful thou art	James Turle 1802–82
Mrs Cecil Frances Alexander 1818–95	Once in royal David's city	H. J. Gauntlett 1805–76
	All things bright and beautiful	trad. arr. Martin Shaw 1875–1958
J. R. Lowell 1819–1891	Once to every man and nation	R. H. Prichard 1811–83
W. Walsham How 1823–97	For all the saints	Ralph Vaughan Williams 1872–1958
Christina Rossetti 1830–94	In the bleak mid-winter	Gustav Holst 1874–1934
C. E. Oakley 1832–65 and NEH editors	Hills of the North, rejoice	Martin Shaw 1875–1958
Phillips Brooks 1835–93	O little town of Bethlehem	trad. English melody, arr. RVW
John Chadwick 1840–1904	Eternal Ruler of the ceaseless round	Orlando Gibbons 1583–1623
Robert Bridges 1844–1930	All my hope on God is founded (after J. Neander)	Herbert Howells 1892–1983
Henry Scott Holland 1847–1918	Judge eternal, throned in splendour	Musical Relicks of Welsh Bards
G. K. Chesterton 1874–1936	O God of earth and altar	trad. English melody, arr. RVW
Eleanor Farjeon 1881–1965	Morning has broken	C. 19th Gaelic melody
African-American spiritual	Were you there when they crucified my Lord?	trad. Spiritual
African-American spiritual	He's got the whole wide world	trad. Spiritual
Caribbean song	The Virgin Mary had a baby boy	trad. Caribbean
Sydney Carter b. 1915	I danced in the morning	trad. Shaker melody
Sebastian Temple 1928–97	Make me a channel of your peace	Sebastian Temple
Taizé Community	Bless the Lord	Jacques Berthier b. 1923

List of hymns

| Iona Community
  John Bell b. 1949
  and Graham Maule
  b. 1958 | We cannot measure
  how you heal | trad. Scottish melody |
| David J. Evans b. 1957 | Be still, for the presence
  of the Lord | David J. Evans b. 1957 |

To the clergy and congregation
of the University Church
of St Mary the Virgin, Oxford

Preface

Many hymns are great poems in their own right – they take us out of the daily round by expressing in images or juxtapositions of ideas those feelings or thoughts which most of us find hard to put into words. They help us to find a divine power within ourselves; they can also inspire worship, action, repentance and faith. But a hymn is more than a great text, the music too needs its own validity. Perhaps the most potent hymn is one where words and melody reinforce each other and which is heard at its best when sung by a congregation in worship.

Hymns, like songs, are powerful communicators. Most hymns spring from a deep personal experience, but it is of their essence that they should be shared in a communal act. They are at once both individual and social. Therefore, to know a little of the personal and cultural context from which they spring greatly enriches what is communicated in an act of congregational singing. It can be argued that historical knowledge of this kind interposes a barrier for a worshipper whose whole being is focused on appropriating these words and music for personal expression or for his/her own needs. We believe that the opposite is true. Strong human emotions of joy and grief, hope and despair, trust and doubt, and, above all, adoration do not change in essence from generation to generation. To relive in the imagination the original experience in which a masterpiece of human self-expression was born creates, in a moment, a new and vivid impact. Eternal realities are ageless but their communication runs like an electric current through successive cultural changes. George Steiner has written about overcoming cultural barriers in understanding a literary text. Meeting a great hymn involves just such an exercise. We need, first, to 'get inside it' by recreating for ourselves the original experience which formed it and by understanding its particular social context. Then, in Steiner's words, we 'bring it home and naturalize' it. But finally we must 'give it back' to its author, for we have no proprietary rights over it: a great hymn transcends all generations and cultures; it is for all times and seasons.[1]

In considering the melding of hymn text with tune we come to a paradox:

---

[1] George Steiner, quoted John Barton, *People of the Book* (SPCK, London, 1988), pp. 62–3, from Steiner, *After Babel: Aspects of Language and Translation* (New York and London, 1975), pp. 296–302.

although some hymns are set to specially composed music, many others have words set to a melody from a source with which there is no immediate connection – a common practice in the performance of popular song. These sources are eclectic: they come from plainsong, psalmodies, folk music, dance tunes, oratorios and art song, all freely adapted where necessary.

As hymn tunes often serve more than one text, the music has usually been given a title, as an easy reference for performers. Often this title has a reference to the tune's origin; for example, the Irish traditional air 'Slane' was chosen as the tune for the English hymn 'Lord of all hopefulness, Lord of all joy' (NEH 239), but it has also now returned to its Celtic roots, as music for the great eighth-century Irish prayer 'Be thou my vision, O Lord of my heart'. This is perhaps where the music, too, has to be 'given back' to its creator so that it may transcend the words with which it was first associated.

No selection of hymns will please everybody. Since ours may be judged too idiosyncratic, we state the guidelines by which we have tried to work. First, we aim, rather ambitiously, at covering, historically, the main periods and chief traditions, with a representative selection of their melodies. Second, we venture onto the doubtful ground of the criteria for choosing 'great' hymns. Third, we have deliberately selected some examples in which a vivid life-story is closely reflected in a particular hymn.

Psalms and Hymns and
Spiritual Songs

Our Book of Psalms derives from a number of earlier collections of Hebrew religious songs, and Christian hymn-singing is rooted in these psalms, as used by Christ and then by the early church. The psalm referred to in Matthew 26:30 would have come from the Hallel, a group of songs including Psalms 113–18, which was sung during the first two nights of the Passover festival. In first-century Jewish worship at home or in the synagogue each verse of a psalm, or a section of it, was intoned by the leader and then repeated by the congregation. (This practical measure continued in most communal religious singing while congregations were unable to read, [see below].) Early Jewish Christians took with them this tradition of antiphonal singing, but not the accompanying musical instruments which, although a major part of temple worship, had, by then, undesirable theatrical associations. St Jerome, like Plato before him, looked severely on the seductive strains of music, writing that a Christian maiden ought not even to know what a lyre or flute looked like. Until the introduction of the organ, said to be by Pope Vitalian in the seventh century, singing in the Western church was unaccompanied.[1]

The earliest Latin psalters were translations from the Greek Septuagint, and the one made by Jerome around 292 AD became the most popular and, eventually, the standard Latin text, though Jerome had gone on to make another translation direct from the original Hebrew. The recitation of the whole psalter over a week became an essential part of the medieval monastic liturgy in the West.

In the sixteenth century, however, the backlash of Protestant reformers to polyphonic music and plainsong psalmody, the exclusive province of clergy and choirs in the Roman church, led to an appropriation of psalm-singing by Reformed congregations. One can see how the cries of an exiled or oppressed Hebrew nation, speaking directly to God in the language of the people, would resonate with Protestants also in exile or facing oppression for their religious beliefs. In the new psalteries (Calvin's first psalter was published in 1538) Latin plainsong was displaced by note-for-syllable metrical psalms. They were often

---

[1] Oxford Comp. to Music, p. 186.

in common or ballad metre, with an ABAB rhyme scheme, and were sung in unison, though, later, simple four-part harmony was introduced, with the melody in the tenor line.

At this time there was a great cross-trade between England, Scotland and Geneva. When Mary Tudor succeeded to the English throne in 1553 a number of Protestant ministers and pastors fearing for their lives – John Hopkins, William Kethe★ and John Knox among them – took refuge in Calvinist Geneva and came back with a new repertoire of psalm verses and musical settings. Although few of their words now survive, we still sing the music of Louis Bourgeois.★

A full version of the psalter soon followed in England. It contained texts and tunes from the Anglo-Genevan psalter of 1556 and from earlier collections edited by Thomas Sternhold (d. 1549) and John Hopkins (d. 1570). This new psalter, published in 1562, became popularly known as 'Sternhold and Hopkins' or, later, the 'Old Version'. In Scotland, the 'Old Psalter', or 'John Knox's Psalter', was published in 1564. Metrical psalms in these and countless succeeding editions and versions, the most important being Nicholas Brady and Nahum Tate's 'New Version' of 1696, continued to be the staple of British public worship for over 200 years. A sixteenth-century engraving shows huge crowds singing metrical psalms at St Paul's Cross in London before King James I and his Court.[1] Congregational singing of metrical psalms was considered so important by the Puritans that in 1644 an Act of Parliament exhorted the minister or clerk 'where many in the congregation cannot read, it is convenient that [he] do read the psalm line by each line before the singing thereof'. This practice became known as 'lining-out' (US: 'deaconing'). It was supposed to be a temporary measure but lingered on to make the singing of psalms often tedious and inimical to sense and musical pitch.[2]

The Church of England continued in the tradition of non-metrical psalm recitation. The *Book of Common Prayer* ordained the recitation of the whole psalter at matins and evensong over a month. Sung to the characteristic nineteenth-century Anglican chant, this practice is still observed in cathedrals and other churches where daily morning and evening prayer take place, but for many people today this regular chanting is outside their experience and the psalms are becoming unfamiliar. Yet many of their images still enrich our imaginations and give expression to our emotions. They come to us partly through the medium of hymns. Such are the shepherd images of Psalm 23★; the longing soul of Psalm 42 in 'As pants the hart for cooling streams' (NEH 337); the grandeur of the universe (Psalm 19) in Addison's★ hymn; the enduring mercies of God (Psalm 136) celebrated by Milton★; the little span of

---

[1] Ibid., p. 493.
[2] Ibid., p. 501.

human life embraced by the sweep of God's timeless care (Psalm 90) which has given us Isaac Watts's majestic hymn★.

In 1834 Henry Francis Lyte★ published *The Spirit of the Psalms* in which he gave a version of a psalm for every Sunday of the church's year. These include 'Praise, my soul, the King of heaven' (Psalm 103) and 'Pleasant are thy Courts above' (Psalm 84). Particularly poignant in human experience from ancient to modern times have been the psalms of slavery and release, exile and return. Thus Psalm 114, 'When Israel went out of Egypt'[2] has inspired poets and musicians in many generations, from Dante's song of the souls released from the tribulations of this world (*Purgatorio*, canto 2) to Samuel Wesley's great anthem★ and modern African-American spirituals. The sighing of exiles finds its most famous expression in Psalm 137, 'By the rivers of Babylon, there we sat down, yea, we wept when we remembered Zion', which in the 1970s was transmuted into a folk song by Don McClean in his album *American Pie*,[1] and later into a pop version by the group Boney M. But Psalm 126 celebrates the opposite experience of the captives' home-coming: 'When the Lord turned again the captivity of Zion, we were like them that dream. Then was our mouth filled with laughter, and our tongue with singing: then said they among the heathen, The Lord hath done great things for them.' Today you can see the whole of this Psalm inscribed on a plaque in St Vitus Cathedral in Prague – for centuries the symbol of frustrated Czech nationhood – with the date of the Velvet Revolution of 1989. At the climax of William Walton's *Belshazzar's Feast* the chorus explodes into a similar celebration of freedom, drawing phrases from Psalms 149 and 150.

Steeped in the psalm tradition of expressing spiritual emotions in song, it is little wonder that, at the high moment of her life, Mary is recorded as bursting into what became the first Christian hymn, the *Magnificat*★. With its theme of joy in God's goodness and his care for the lowly, this song echoes many phrases from both psalms and prophetic writings, but particularly Hannah's song of thanksgiving for her son in I Samuel 2:1–10. In Luke's Gospel the *Magnificat* is paired with Zacharias's song which we know as the *Benedictus* ('Blessed be the Lord God of Israel, for he hath visited and redeemed his people') (Luke 1:68–79). Luke puts a further song into the mouth of old Simeon in 2:29–32: 'Lord, now lettest thou thy servant depart in peace ...', known to us as the *Nunc Dimittis*. Here, too, Old Testament echoes are apparent, especially from the 'servant theology' of Isaiah 40–55. These two canticles had become an integral part of the church's worship by around the fourth century. In England their themes have been an inspiration to many poets and musicians. Most English composers since the Reformation have

---

[1] Don McLean, *American Pie* (United Artists, 1971).
[2] Quotations from Psalms in this paragraph are from the Authorized Version.

written settings to these two canticles which are central to the Anglican service of evensong. At an unknown early date the *Gloria* and the *Te Deum* also became part of Christian worship.

In the words of the title given to this chapter, St Paul encouraged Christian congregations to sing psalms and hymns and spiritual songs, and scholars have identified traces of such hymns in the epistles. If the teaching manual known as the *Didache*★ is as early as the first century, as scholars now think, the oldest complete hymn, after the New Testament canticles, which we still sing, connects us with the worship of unknown first-century congregations. St Clement of Alexandria, in the course of his teaching on Christian discipline, preserved the text of a hymn beginning 'Bridle of colts untamed'. The text of a beautiful evening hymn, *Phos Hilaron*★, is dated now as before the fourth century. By this time a different use for hymns appears when the church was split by the Arian controversy[1] about the nature of Christ. When the Arians were forbidden to hold public worship in Constantinople they chanted religious songs in the streets. St John Chrysostom organized counter-processions of hymn-singers, rather in the style of rival football-slogan shouters today. Indeed, similar practices can still happen during religious celebrations in the Church of the Holy Sepulchre in Jerusalem.

According to St Augustine, it was St Ambrose, Bishop of Milan (c. 340–97) who introduced, from the Eastern church, the regular use of hymns sung in church services outside the liturgy of the Mass. These were sung to a type of metrical plainsong which was mainly syllabic, to make the understanding of the Latin words easier. His best-known hymn is *Deus creator omnium* – 'Creator of the earth and sky', in C. Bigg's translation (NEH 152). We have contemporary words of many of these hymns but their melodies have come down to us only since early medieval times, when Guido of Arezzo's great invention of the 1020s, a four-lined stave which gave notes a fixed pitch, meant that music could be notated and written down in a standardized form. Broadly speaking, by the early Middle Ages in the West, we can distinguish two types of hymn: processionals for the church's high festivals and commemorations of saints, in which the whole lay community would probably participate, and 'office' hymns, so called because they were used in monastic 'offices', the services which punctuated the monastic day (e.g. lauds, sext, vespers etc.). These were mainly scripturally based and objective in tone, characterized by a 'threadbare sobriety'.[2]

But by the twelfth century a more personal type of 'spiritual song' was beginning to appear, a manifestation of a growing 'humanistic' individualism. This is seen, for instance, in a new emphasis on the cult of the Virgin Mary at a

---

[1] Routley, *Hymns*, p. 26.
[2] Ibid, pp. 29, 204.

personal level from which sprang the use of the *Ave Maria* based on the salutations of Gabriel and Elizabeth in Luke ch. 1. Again, expressing this increasingly individual devotion, an unknown author wrote *Jesu dulcis memoria* ('Jesu, the very thought of thee'), which was formerly ascribed to Bernard of Clairvaux but is now thought, possibly, to have been written by a French nun (NEH 385, tr. Edward Caswall★).[1] Abelard's★ collection of hymns for Heloise constitutes a third example. A long personal poem such as Bernard of Cluny's *De contemptu mundi*★ was not intended for worship, but from it J. M. Neale★ culled a number of hymns. The best known of these, 'Jerusalem the Golden', like Abelard's *O quanta qualia*★, imagines the longed-for paradise.

The movement for personal devotion led naturally to a more direct participation of the laity in spiritual exercises, especially among the rising bourgeois class of Italian and French cities. By the early thirteenth century the laity were seeking their own forms of religious association, such as the Humiliati in Lombardy and the Waldenses in Lyons. Pious fraternities created their own religious celebrations outside the liturgy, drawing on contemporary dance and song. An early-thirteenth-century manuscript has preserved the 'Prose of the Ass', a text written for a procession commemorating the Flight into Egypt. The tune, known today as *Orientis Partibus*, is now set to an Easter hymn (NEH 105).[2] Ecstatic movements of religious fervour swept the towns on a number of occasions. The 'Year of the Great Alleluia', 1233, was described by the Franciscan chronicler Salimbene as a time of praise and jubilation, when holy *laude* were sung by nobles and people, citizens and country folk, and every parish wanted its own street procession.[3] These *laude* were free compositions, outside the Office-Hymn tradition, often in the vernacular. In the mid-thirteenth century, processions of Flagellants sang them spontaneously as they moved from town to town. The *Dies Irae*★, put together at this time, and the so-called 'Canticle of the Sun'★, composed by St Francis, were probably of this genre. From the fourteenth century we have a hymn by Bianco of Siena★ which may have been a *lauda* written for his fraternity, the *Gesuati*. By this time the singing of *laude* had developed into marching songs of crowds, with rhythms and tunes appropriated from secular ballads. At Cortona and Urbino, songbooks of such groups (often known as *disciplinati*) survived. The tradition continued well into the eighteenth century. Dr Burney, in the account of his travels in Italy, describes the celebrated *Laudisti* processing outside the cathedral in Florence, carrying lighted tapers and singing 'a cheerful hymn in three parts, which they executed very well'.[3]

---

[1] Ibid., p. 29.
[2] Quoted G. Peck, *The Fool of God – Jacopone da Todi* (University of Alabama Press, Alabama, 1980), p. 64, from Salimbene, OM, *Cronaca*, MGHS, xxxii, pp. 22–4.
[3] *Oxford Comp. to Music*, p. 989.

A striking example of a secular song, the melody of which became the basis for liturgical music, occurs in the case of the popular marching song *L'homme armé* used in at least 31 mass settings of which two by Josquin des Près (c. 1500) are among the best known (recorded by the Tallis Scholars on Gimell CDGIM 019).[1]

The master of the *lauda* in Italy was Jacopone da Todi (c. 1230–1306), a Franciscan who retained the lay status of the Third Order.[2] His outpourings of spiritual verse in the vernacular are very personal and it is not clear how much of this was intended for public use, but several of his *laude* appear in extant songbooks and, for one at least, *O Christe omnipotente*, the music has survived. A series of poems, *Donna del Paradiso*, is in dramatic form and possibly formed part of the widespread devotion of *disciplinati* to the cult of the Virgin Mary. Here is one verse of Mary's lament, calling on nature to share her grief:

Planga la terra, Planga lo mare,	The earth grieves, the sea grieves,
Planga lo pesce ke sa notare,	The fish grieve who know how to swim,
Plangan le bestie nel pascolare,	The animals grieve in their pasture,
Plangan l'aucelli nel lor volare.	The birds grieve as they fly.
(Peck, 141)	(Trans. M. E. Reeves)

The guild initiative in England, which led to the development of medieval mystery plays, involved the use of secular music, including the carol, and dance for religious devotion. While hymns take us through the liturgical year in a serious manner, carols, in folk or ballad style, add a touch of sparkle and sometimes irreverence as they describe the events of the Bible, including the great festivals of Christmas and Easter. They often have a domestic quality: we hear of the doubts of Joseph when he hears that his affianced wife is pregnant, of the child to be born not in 'housen nor in hall ... but in an ox's stall', of 'sweet Jesus' asking his mother if he can go to play at the holy well. In the many Christmas Eve wassail songs the singers look forward to a good bowl of spiced ale at the local manor house while a north of England version also begs for 'your mouldy cheese and some of your Christmas loaf'![3]

Several of the narrative carols are based on Christian legends such as the three ships 'sailing in on Christmas day', which were said to have carried the holy skulls of the three wise men from Byzantium to their resting place in Cologne. One of the most beautiful and mystical of such carols is an accumulative song which refers to Christ as the wounded knight of mythology (with echoes of the legend of the Holy Grail) and to the celebration of the

---

[1] We owe this reference to Dr Amanda Collins.

[2] See Peck, *op. cit.* for the life and *laude* of Jacopone. Recently the tradition of ecstatic *laude* has been revived by Amelia Cuni, an Indian musician who has used Jacopone's poems for her *danza d'amore*, bringing together Indian mysticism and Western medieval spirituality.

[3] Erik Routley, *The English Carol* (Herbert Jenkins, London, 1958) p. 70.

Eucharist. The final verse also alludes to the Glastonbury thorn (see William Blake★). The earliest text, without music, was discovered in the *Commonplace Book of Richard Hill*, a mayor of London, c. 1504. The verses below, collected from north Staffordshire, are those that are usually sung:

> Over yonder's a park, which is newly begun:
> *All bells of Paradise I heard them a-ring:*
> Which is silver on the outside and gold within:
> *And I love sweet Jesus above all thing.*
>
> And in that park there stands a hall:
> Which is covered all over with purple and pall:
>
> And in that hall there stands a bed:
> Which is hung all round with silk curtains so red:
>
> And in that bed there lies a knight:
> Whose wounds they do bleed by day and by night:
>
> At that bedside there lies a stone:
> Which our blest Virgin Mary knelt upon:
>
> At that bed's head there grows a thorn:
> Which was never so blossomed since Christ was born.[1]

A common feature of many such carols is their stanza-and-chorus format, where the story or message is pointed by a refrain. Sometimes this can be a repetitive phrase such as 'Noel, Noel!', 'Alleluia' or 'Gloria in excelsis deo!', but usually there is a full chorus, as in the Sans Day Carol:

> *And Mary bore Jesus Christ our Saviour for to be.*
> *And the first tree in the greenwood, it was the holly, holly, holly.*
> *And the first tree in the greenwood, it was the holly!*

Erik Routley[2] suggests that this type of carol, though not itself a dance form, had its roots in outdoor processional dances where the chorus provided the leader with a pause for breath in his storytelling (the word 'stanza' comes from the Latin *stare*, to stand). They usually have a strong beat and, unlike the even-paced metre of a typical hymn, carols are often in compound (6/8) or triple time, where one can feel the foot stamping or tapping out the pulse – as in 'Now the hólly bears a bérry' or ' Quém pastóres laúdavére' – or they are in a strong duple metre such as the Burgundian carol, 'Gúillaume prénds ton támbourín' (Willie take your little drum).

Another genre of carol has a more intimate and personal nature, often like the *laude* sung in devotion to Christ or the Virgin Mary. There are several

---

[1] *Oxford Book of Carols* (1964), no. 184.
[2] Routley, *The English Carol*, p. 28.

lullaby carols such as the processional 'Song of the Nuns of Chester', c. 1425 (OBC 67), and 'The Coventry Carol'★, which was sung in the cycle of pageants staged by the Shearmen and Tailors of Coventry in the fifteenth century. These religious dramas gave a chance for villains and comics, the Herods and the devils, to rant and rage on stage in true melodramatic style (hence Hamlet's reference to 'out-Heroding Herod'). But though they may have had some of the best lines, the Christ-child and his story still kept the most moving tunes.

With this inheritance of medieval lay religious practices it is little wonder that the Reformation Protestant congregations soon began to sing hymns in the vernacular. In the early sixteenth century, followers of the Czech reformer Jan Hus (1369–1415) compiled the first congregational hymn-books, using secular airs and newly composed tunes. Martin Luther (1483–1546) published his first chorale songbook in 1524[1] and these, together with the metrical psalters, eventually reprogrammed the whole practice of Protestant and, later, Roman Catholic religious worship in Europe and America.

English churches, which followed Calvinist rather than Lutheran practices, were at first reluctant to admit anything but the singing of psalms in metrical chant during public worship. It must be remembered that George Herbert's religious poems, for instance, only came into use as hymns much later. It was the great resolve of Isaac Watts★, in the early eighteenth century, to find a more common expression of religious fervour, followed by the outburst of Wesleyan hymnody★, that opened the way to the richness and variety of modern English hymns. In 1737 John Wesley's *Collection of Psalms and Hymns* made its first appearance. From the eighteenth century onwards nonconformist worship was being enriched by hymn-writers such as Philip Doddridge (1702–51), the Congregational minister of Castle Street Church, Northampton, who wrote about 370 hymns.

Yet for Anglican churches, hymn-singing in the eighteenth and early nineteenth centuries was still unofficial, indeed technically illegal within the prescribed liturgy of the Prayer Book. It was, however, infiltrating through use at evangelical prayer-meetings of the type encouraged by John Newton★. His Olney hymn-book appeared in 1779. In fact, between 1801 and 1820, 42 hymn-books for Anglicans were published. In 1819 the singing of hymns in Anglican services was challenged in the York Consistory Court but the Archbishop approved a special selection and, gradually, hymns became legalized, first in the northern province and then generally. By this time 'lining-out' had gradually been replaced by a choir with organ accompaniment in town and city churches or, in country areas, a small instrumental band often placed with the singers in the west gallery. Thomas Hardy gives vivid

---

[1] *Oxford Comp. to Music*, p. 498.

descriptions of such bands in *Under the Greenwood Tree* and *The Mayor of Casterbridge*. But this still gave the congregation a mainly passive role. This was no longer to the liking of Victorian clergy and hymn-writers. By the mid-nineteenth century the Victorian enthusiasm for composing and translating hymns was in full flood.

Their enthusiasm was partly stimulated by competition with the popular hymn-singing of nonconformist chapels where the whole congregation could join in rousing tunes, whereas in many Anglican services participation was largely limited to the choir chanting the psalms. In 1802, John Venn, rector of Clapham and a leading evangelical, wrote: 'I am persuaded that the singing has been a great instrument in the Dissenters' hands of drawing away persons from the Church and why should we not take that instrument out of their hands?'[1] There was also the view in some quarters that too many of the nonconformist hymns were focused solely on personal subjective devotions. This was particularly a criticism made by High Church Anglicans who wanted hymn-singing to be directly related to the church's liturgy and the seasons of the liturgical year. At first they were reluctant to admit anything but ancient hymns – an extreme example was J. M. Neales's *Hymnal Noted* of 1851, consisting entirely of Office Hymns taken mainly from medieval Sarum plainsong manuscripts for the secular (non-monastic) rites of Salisbury Cathedral. However, by the mid-century, Anglo-Catholics and, later, Roman Catholics were following their evangelical brethren in the great work of composing or translating the hymns that would democratize parish worship by bringing it alive.

The publications of hymn-books became a major religious 'industry' in the nineteenth century. Each denomination published its own congregational selection, coloured by its particular theology and often making its own particular selection of tunes. Wesleyan Methodists retained the 1780 edition of Wesley's book, with additions. Primitive Methodists published their own in 1825. Particular Baptists got their own hymnal in 1828, while the more liberal Baptist wing adopted the *General Baptist Hymn Book*, published in 1830. From 1836, Congregational churches used the *Congregational Church Hymn Book* as a supplement to Isaac Watts's* *Psalms and Hymns*. For a general congregational hymn-book Anglicans had to wait until the publication of *Hymns Ancient and Modern*, edited by Henry Baker and W. H. Monk*, in 1860/1.

For this new venture, the editors commissioned material from hymn-writers and prominent composers of the day. These included Samuel Wesley, Arthur Sullivan, Henry Monk himself, J. B. Dykes and F. Gore Ouseley. In the music edition of *A&M*, published in 1861, words and music were printed on the same page. This was an important decision because tunes – especially

---

[1] Bradley, *Abide with Me*, p. 15.

the new ones – became associated with specific texts. The supplement to Tate and Brady's psalter of 1709 had left the choice of melody to the discretion of the organist or choir-master, who would know a tune by its title, e.g. *York, Windsor, St David's, St Ann's* (sic), *Southwell*, and its metrical category, SM (short metre), CM (common metre) and so on. (The supplement also suggested special tunes for 'psalms of praise and cheerfulness' and 'penitential or mournful psalms'.)[1] It was then a simple matter to match the metre with an appropriate tune. *Hymns Ancient and Modern* ousted some common choices: for instance Nahum Tate's 'While shepherds watched their flocks by night' had been sung to a variety of melodies, but Monk chose *Winchester Old* from Este's *Psalter* of 1592 and his selection has prevailed. This model has generally been followed by other hymn-book editors, but often with a different choice of music. We can now sing a hymn such as 'Lead kindly light'★ to its original *A&M* tune by Dykes (1823–76) or to the one most commonly used by C. H. Purday (1799–1885) or to a third setting by W. H. Harris (1883–1973). The words edition of *A&M* was soon bound together with the *Book of Common Prayer*, and the hymnal had no Anglican rival until *The English Hymnal* appeared in 1906.

There were many more hymn or song collections produced by Victorians, often written for children and young people. It was part of an explosion of music in every walk of life: in festivals, schools, the parlour (one in ten Victorian households had a piano), the public house and the music hall. Much of this had a moral intent. John Spencer Curwen, writing of his father's tonic sol-fa system, printed in contemporary songbooks and sheet music, says: 'The method was an indirect means of aiding worship, temperance and culture ... of reforming character, of spreading Christianity. The artistic aspect of the work done by the sol-fa method is indeed less prominent than its moral and religious influence.'[2]

The English Hymnal of 1906 had the high aim of being 'a collection of the best hymns in the English language' drawn from all religious sources. It should, however, be noted that here, as in hymn-books of all periods, editors felt free to adapt, rearrange or add to their original texts in a quite cavalier manner.[3] The book's musical editor, Ralph Vaughan Williams, steeped both in the English folk tradition and the music of the church, made musical excellence a moral issue and chose familiar melodies that had stood the test of time rather than opting for 'specially composed tunes – that bane of many a hymnal', and

---

[1] Supplement to Tate and Brady, *A New Version of the Psalms of David*, 1709.

[2] Dave Russell, *Popular Music in England 1840–1914: A Social History* (Manchester University Press, 1997), p. 23.

[3] For example, Milton's paraphrase of Psalms 82, 85 and 86 are amalgamated into 'The Lord will come and not be slow' (NEH 15) by selective verses as follows: v. 1: Ps. 85:73 adapted; v.2: Ps. 85:11; v. 3: Ps. 82:7; v. 4: Ps: 86:9; v. 5: Ps. 86:10.

---

wrote that 'there are already many hundreds of fine tunes in existence, so many indeed that it is impossible to include more than a small part of them in any one collection.'[1] Vaughan Williams also preferred to go back, where possible, to the original version of tunes by Gibbons or Bourgeois, adding only 'mean' or inner parts as necessary.

The first Roman Catholic hymn-book, the *Westminster Hymnal*, appeared in 1912. There have been many revisions of denominational hymn-books in the late nineteenth and twentieth centuries. The Congregational book was revised in 1881, 1916 and 1951. The United Reformed Church published an entirely new book, *Rejoice and Sing*, in 1991. The *Baptist Church Hymnal* appeared in 1900. The *Methodist Hymn Book*, published in 1904, has been revised as *Hymns and Psalms: A Methodist Ecumenical Hymn Book* (1983). An important development in widening the range of hymns from many sources was Robert Bridges' *Yattendon Hymnal*★ (1895–9).

In 1925 two of the original editors of *The English Hymnal*, Percy Dearmer and Vaughan Williams, were responsible, with Martin Shaw, for a more forward-looking hymn-book, *Songs of Praise*. It was intended to be international in outlook, including 'a full expression of that faith which is common to the English-speaking peoples of today, both in the Commonwealth and the United States'.[2] It was also aimed at a younger audience. *Songs of Praise* follows the general pattern of the earlier *EH* but, in an important new emphasis, transferred to the 'General' section most of the hymns about the life of Christ, so that they could be sung throughout the church year and thus displace some of the overworked penitential themes. Again, the editors made a point of 'recovering old tunes of exceptional vigour and beauty' and finding lyrics of poetic quality. Cecil Spring-Rice's 'I vow to thee my country', set to the middle section of *Jupiter* from Gustav Holst's *The Planets* and Blake's *Jerusalem* are two of these. In many ways *Songs of Praise* was transitional in its move away from organizing hymns largely around the liturgical year. Its section on 'social service' introduces an important note. Social issues were already finding expression in the nineteenth century. Some of the most remarkable publications were those which demonstrate that collective singing as a binding activity could be copied by groups outside the churches. Thus, Robert Owen's disciples nourished their identity through *Social Hymns for the Use of Friends of the Rational System of Society*, published in 1850, while *Hymns of Progress* (1883) was popular with ethical groups.

In the latter half of the nineteenth century there was a significant development of hymn-writing centred on social issues, sparked off by the desperate hunger of the 1840s and fuelled by Christian socialism. This was

---

[1] *The English Hymnal* (OUP, Oxford, 1906), Preface, p. iii.
[2] *Songs of Praise* (OUP, Oxford, 1925), Preface, p. iii.

heralded in 1840 by Ebenezer Elliott's passionate hymn, set to music by Joseph Booth:[1]

> When wilt Thou save the people,
>   O God of mercy, when?
> The people, Lord, the people!
>   Not thrones and crowns, but men!

Large mass rallies for those untouched by the churches became a major social instrument used by Victorian evangelists. William Booth wrote gospel songs for the Salvation Army, the army of Christ marching to save the inner cities. In the early 1870s Moody and Sankey brought their American-style rallies to big city halls in England.[2] Moody was the preacher while Sankey seems to have been the Victorian equivalent of a pop singer. Music was a major 'weapon' in evangelizing. Sankey could improvise tunes, accompanying himself on the organ. He would sing a moving emotional solo and then announce a rousing gospel chorus which carried the audience to a high pitch. One of the favourites which always appeared first in editions of their *Sacred Songs and Solos* was 'Ho! My comrades, see the signal'. The story behind this was that in the American Civil War, General Sherman sent a semaphore message to a hard-besieged depot in Georgia: 'Hold the fort for I am coming.' Another American, P. P. Bliss, made this the basis for the splendid battle-song which became the theme cry of Moody and Sankey's crusades. It even found a place in the original *English Hymnal* (EH 570) and is best remembered for its chorus:

> 'Hold the fort for I am coming',
> Jesus signals still;
> Wave the answer back to heaven,
> 'By thy grace we will!'[3]

During the period of the American Civil War and the campaign for the abolition of slavery there was a powerful liberal movement which often expressed itself in poems and hymns. Julia Ward Howe's hymn, 'Mine eyes have seen the glory of the coming of the Lord', was inspired by a visit to the army camp of the Potomac in 1861 where she heard the popular song 'John Brown's body lies a-mouldering in the grave, but his soul goes marching on'. She adapted the tune with its chorus 'Glory, glory Hallelujah' to her new

---

[1] Elliott, from Rotherham, became a leading Chartist. His hymn was first published in a Sheffield newspaper in 1832 and was used at many Chartist rallies; see Bradley, *Abide with Me*, p. 125.

[2] Ibid., pp. 178–9, where Bradley gives a vivid picture of a Moody & Sankey rally. One of the authors of this book remembers many of their songs, as sung in the early twentieth century, especially the relish of thumping out 'Hold the fort' and the lingering sentimentality of 'Tell me the old, old story'.

[3] Ibid., p. 173.

words. The American Unitarian Samuel Johnson (1822–82) wrote 'City of God, how broad and far outspread thy walls sublime!' (NEH 346) in 1864. J. R. Lowell★ and John Chadwick★ both wrote hymns of social aspiration for special occasions. In Britain, Henry Scott Holland★ and G. K. Chesterton★ were expressing similar ideals which gave an eloquent voice to the developing social conscience of Christians.

But it is when we get into this field of social, national and missionary hymns that we meet problems. Some are too optimistic for our *fin de siècle* outlook. Johnson's hymn (quoted above) perhaps falls under this judgement with its vision of progress: 'How grandly hath thine empire grown of freedom, love and truth! ... How rise thy towers, serene and bright, to meet the dawning day!' (NEH 346). Similarly, the aspirations of 'Thy kingdom come! on bended knee the passing ages pray', by Frederick Hosmer (1840–1929), create difficulties with their unwavering expectation of the day 'When knowledge, hand in hand with peace, shall walk the earth abroad. The day of perfect righteousness, the promised day of God' (NEH 500). Belief in steady, invincible progress was even more clearly expressed in a poem by J. Addington Symonds (1840–93) which was not written as a hymn but was seized upon as a vision of the future by early twentieth-century optimists.[1] It was a favourite with students, appearing in *Songs of Praise* in 1931, and, in a slightly different form, found a place in *Congregational Praise* in 1951 (no. 583). The text demonstrates how far we have moved since it was written:

> These things shall be! A loftier race
> Than e'er the world hath known, shall rise
> With flame of freedom in their souls
> And light of science in their eyes.
>
> They shall be gentle, brave and strong
> To spill no drop of blood, but dare
> All that may plant man's lordship firm
> On earth and fire and sea and air.
>
> They shall be simple in their homes
> And splendid in their public ways,
> Filling the mansions of the state
> With music and with hymns of praise.
>
> Nation with nation, land with land,
> Unarmed shall live as comrades free;
> In every heart and brain shall throb
> The pulse of one fraternity.

---

[1] The verses selected for the hymn were taken from Symonds's poem 'A vista' which was published in his *New and Old: A Volume of Verse, 1880*. The original has 15 verses. We owe this reference to Dr Elaine Kaye.

> New arts shall bloom of loftier mould,
> And mightier music thrill the skies,
> And every life shall be a song,
> When all the earth is paradise.
>
> (From *Songs of Praise*, 312)

Congregational Praise substitutes 'knowledge' for 'science' in verse one, omits verse three and adds two other verses.

Among the Victorians, Mrs Alexander★ was the outstanding writer of hymns for children. A few of these are still favourites but she raises for us problems not only concerning the social environment but also in our different concepts of childhood.

Kipling's 'Recessional', written for Queen Victoria's Diamond Jubilee in 1897, is a fascinating study of the tension between a celebration of the British Empire and a call to national penitence for all our boasting (EH 558). Understandably, it has been dropped from the *New English Hymnal* but it has a lesson to teach and we ought to revive a modified version of it. The problem with some early missionary hymns lies in the heroic but uncompromising psychology of the first generation of missionaries, most of whom saw the situation of the 'heathen' in stark terms of black and white. We can no longer stomach Bishop Heber's picture in 'From Greenland's icy mountains' (EH 547) of a world where 'every prospect pleases and only man is vile'; where the gifts of God are lavishly bestowed but 'The heathen in his blindness bows down to wood and stone'. Similarly, 'Hills of the North, rejoice!', by C. E. Oakley★ (1832–65), has been banished, but its splendid imagery and tune have brought a reprieve in the form of a much-revised version with a clear vision of God as the Creator and Sustainer of *all* peoples on the earth (NEH 7)★. We need some more new-style hymns for a multicultural society in a global village.

In general our difficulties with hymns that are now culturally unacceptable apply only to this fairly recent category of hymns devoted to a social vision in a secular world. By contrast, hymns of worship, of theological teaching and personal spirituality seem to make a timeless impact; although clothed in the cultural imagery of their own day, they speak with a universal and unchanging voice.

Post-Second World War collections have introduced many more contemporary hymns and worship songs which have a social gospel to preach, among them material from national and religious communities. From African-Americans and the Caribbean islands come the great gospel songs and spirituals which echo the cry of the oppressed throughout history: 'Let my people go!' In the 1960s, folk-singers such as Sydney Carter★, with their catchy tunes and rhythms, brought in a sense of dance and fun – and the guitar. The ecumenical Taizé★ movement has given us a renewed spirituality in worship, while the songs of the Iona Community* in Scotland use Scottish ballads with new words to bring relevance to their mission to severely deprived neighbourhoods. And, finally, the Charismatic movement has established itself in the forefront of worship song. All these strands are reflected in books such as the United Reformed Church's *Rejoice and Sing* of 1991, with over 100 hymns by living writers including David J. Evans*, Gerard Markland and Graham Kendrick. Modern editors have also taken steps to use inclusive language and positive and appropriate images, avoiding militarism and triumphalism because, in the words of the editors of *Hymns Old and New* 'history, including current events, shows only too clearly the misuse to which those images are open'.[1] In this collection, as in the Evangelical *New Mission Praise* (Marshall Pickering, 1996), now the most widely used hymn-book in Britain, hymns and songs are printed in alphabetical order, with suggestions only at the end for liturgical, social or spiritual occasions. This was also the practice in Kevin Mayhew's earlier *Celebration Hymnal* (Mayhew-McCrimmon, 1976), published in response to the Second Vatican Council's demand for vernacular worship in Roman Catholic churches.[2] The books were also set out in a form that could be copied and used under licence (see below).

There are, however, exceptions to this trend. The editors of *Hymns Ancient and Modern, New Standard Version* (1983) and the revised *New English Hymnal* (1986) still retain the layout of earlier editions and offer an accompaniment to the liturgy throughout the church's year. *The New English Hymnal* includes most of the great classic hymns in common use together with a few post-war hymns. However, the editors 'regard much of [the new writing] as poor in quality and ephemeral in expression ... We have not overlooked the social duty of Christians, but we believe ... [it] can often be better expressed in sermons and prayers than in hymnody.'[3]

Nevertheless, the trend continues. In the last 25 years the folk and popular music movement has developed, along with wider changes in worship: the altar is placed within the body of the church, preaching is more informal and conversational and hymn-singing is often accompanied by guitars, keyboard etc. instead of an organ (most new hymnals are printed with guitar chords as well as four-part harmony). Music editions are no longer geared to trained treble voices, but print tunes in lower keys and different harmonies more suited to a general congregation. And, while many churches still provide individual books, there is a new and important trend in modern church worship. It began in the United States as a way of regulating the use of

---

[1] *Hymns Old and New* (Kevin Mayhew, Bury St Edmunds, 1996).

[2] This has now been superseded by *Liturgical Hymns Old and New* (Kevin Mayhew, Bury St Edmunds, 1999).

[3] *New English Hymnal* (Canterbury Press, Norwich, 1988), Preface, p. vi.

copyright hymns and may perhaps replace the hymn-book as we know it. Churches and schools can now select their music for worship under a special licensing scheme, from CCL Christian Copyright Licensing (Europe), which was set up in 1991. Its mission is to 'encourage the spirit of worship through music ... spontaneously, conveniently, affordably, and legally'.[1] In this way, churches can build up their own databases to use in overhead projection or to make up purpose-built service books.

Today, a new world of information and communications technology – the global village – can take us anywhere in the world in religious terms. Through radio, television or the Internet, the Shiloah Baptist Church of down-town Washington, DC can share its Sunday preacher and magnificent gospel choir with listeners in Chipping Campden, Gloucestershire and Sydney, Australia. Christians under threat in South America can take comfort and be uplifted by the exuberant dancing and singing of open-air multi-faith gatherings, such as the World Council of Churches, in Zimbabwe, in 1998. Churches of all denominations publish on websites their most meaningful events and sermons. The ease with which new hymns and new forms of liturgy can be compiled, printed and disseminated may mean either that the common ground cracks apart between worshippers or that we can share our faith in a way that would have been beyond the imagination of the early hymn-writers. But, of course, new hymn and worship song-books are still being published. Two of the latest are the evangelical *Sing Glory* (Kevin Mayhew, 1999), with an associated CD, and *Songs for the New Millennium* (Methodist Publishing House, 1999) which offers a book that can be photocopied and a floppy disk with the words of the songs. Both look forward to a future for our hymns.

Hymns form a great social bond between the past and the present, while looking to the future. When we sing hymns that spark us off, 'a real meeting of minds has occurred across what may be a great cultural divide and there is something new in the world'.[2]

---

[1] *Congregational Worship and Copyright* (CCLI, Eastbourne, 2000), Mission Statement.
[2] Quoted in Barton, *People of the Book* (SPCK, 1988), p. 63.

TRANSLATORS

Many favourite hymns would be denied to English worshipping congregations today were it not for the work of enthusiastic translators and musicians. There have been a number of these but several stand out for their contributions.

E. Caswall (1814–78) was one of the energetic group of High Churchmen who set out to rescue hymn-singing from the subjectivity which they condemned in so many Victorian hymns. He believed that the only satisfactory hymns were the Latin office hymns designed 'to take the individual out of himself; to set before him . . . all the varied and sublime objects of the faith and to blend him with the universal Family of the Faithful.'[1] To the task of translation, therefore, he devoted the literary gifts which earlier had won him the university prize for poetry at Oxford. His *Lyra Catholica* (1849) gave the hymns for Vespers, Compline and Benediction. By this time he had joined Newman at the Birmingham Oratory. When, with J. M. Neale, he translated Aquinas's eucharistic hymn, *Pange, lingua, gloriosi corporis mysterium*, he was accused of going beyond what the Anglican church would stand for, yet he still had 21 hymn translations in the 1875 edition of *Hymns Ancient and Modern*. The first editors of *The English Hymnal* selected eleven of his translations. The best know of these is 'Jesus, the very thought of thee', which was then believed to be by St Bernard of Clairvaux★.

J. M. Neale (1818–66) was a Tractarian High Churchman who, for much of his career, was Warden of Sackville College, East Grinstead, since he was barred from a parish living by his bishop, who objected to his ritualistic practices. But his contribution in original hymns and translations was remarkable – it accounted for more than one tenth of the first *English Hymnal* – and his translation of many early hymns from Greek and Latin reconnected our worship with the spirituality of the Orthodox and early Latin churches.

Robert Bridges (1844–1936)★ brought a different kind of emphasis to his selection of hymns for translation. In youth he had been attracted to High Church practices, but in maturity he took a more humanistic position, less concerned with dogmatic belief than with reconciling scientific knowledge with Christian faith and with beauty in the words and music of Christian worship. While living at Yattendon (Berkshire) he produced the *Yattendon Hymnal*★ (1895–9) with the aim of bringing into use earlier hymns and melodies which were unknown or forgotten. These included not only ancient examples but more recent translations from German Lutheran hymns. Together with Percy Dearmer and Vaughan Williams he exercised a considerable influence on the choice of hymns and tunes in *The English Hymnal* and other hymn-books.

---

[1] Bradley, *Abide with Me*, p. 199.

Catherine Winkworth (1827–78) was one of an interesting group of Victorian women who devoted much time to opening up the riches of German hymnody in its classic period to English congregations. She was a Broad Church woman – James Martineau, Charles Kingsley and F. D. Maurice were her friends – who was also a pioneer in higher education for women. She and her sister spent substantial periods in Germany. Baron von Bunsen, Prussian minister in London, encouraged her translating work which she published in two parts as *Lyra Germanica* between 1841 and 1854. This was intended for use in private devotion but her hymns were soon seized upon by compilers of the main hymn-books. A distinctive feature of her work was that she also introduced the great German chorale tunes, producing *The Chorale Book for England* with melodies edited by Mendelssohn's pupil W. Sterndale Bennett. Her best-known translations are 'Now thank we all our God'★ and 'Praise to the Lord, the Almighty'.

Among other translators of hymns selected here were John Cosin★ (1594–1672), a Cambridge Platonist, Thomas Helmore★, and R. F. Littledale, a nineteenth-century Anglican cleric who had to retire, for reasons of ill health, from St Mary the Virgin, Soho, and spent the rest of his life in the country, writing and translating hymns.

COMPOSERS AND ARRANGERS

Louis Bourgeois★ (1510–61), a French Huguenot, was a great musician of the Calvinist reformation, one of a team whom Calvin brought to Geneva to provide words and music – some specially composed, some from other sources – for his new French-language metrical psalms and canticles. Bourgeois, like Calvin, gave an enduring French style to English and Scottish worship. Marian refugees such as Kethe★ studied under him and included his melodies in their English-language psalters. Today, most of those English words are forgotten, but we still sing Bourgeois's melodies to six hymns in the NEH. One of these, originally set for Psalm 86, is for Bishop R. Heber's hymn, 'Virgin-born, we bow before thee' (NEH 187). Like so much of Bourgeois's music it carries an emotional weight that goes to the heart of the Christian faith.

Orlando Gibbons★ (1583–1625) was court organist for James I and choirmaster of the Children of the Chapel Royal. He wrote for viols and virginals and was considered 'the best finger' or keyboard player of his age. His main *oeuvre* is his church music: settings for the Eucharist, anthems such as David's lament for his father, 'When David heard that Absalom was slain', and, of course, hymn music. Gibbons's madrigals include the beautiful 'The Silver Swan', heard to its most ravishing effect when sung out-of-doors on the water. He died suddenly in 1625 on the occasion when the new king, Charles I, summoned the whole Court, including members of the Chapel Royal, to Canterbury to greet his French bride, Henrietta Maria.

Ralph Vaughan Williams (1872–1958) was a man of great warmth and breadth of vision. He considered himself a Londoner but his music brings the fresh voice of the Gloucestershire countryside to our hymn-books. He was a key figure in the twentieth-century revival of English music, enjoying both folk song, which he considered the true music of the people, and the more cultivated notes of Tudor and Jacobean composers. Both elements are reflected in hymn melodies of our collection. When he became music editor of *The English Hymnal* in 1906, he saw it his main task to include the finest specimens of every style of music, going back to the best early version of psalm and hymn tunes and throwing out the 'excesses of Victoriana'.[1] His influence still permeates *The New English Hymnal*, where 35 tunes are written or arranged by him. Folk-song melodies include a Warwickshire ballad for 'Firmly I believe and truly' (p. 149) and the traditional *Forest Green* for the Christmas, song so loved by children, 'O little town of Bethlehem'. It was RVW who brought the tunes of Gibbons★, Tallis, Henry Lawes★ and William Croft to our hymnals. His own best-known tune is perhaps *Down Ampney*, named after his native Cotswold village, for 'Come down, O Love Divine'. His other work ranges from the folk idiom of 'Linden Lea' to his powerful wartime Sixth Symphony, his ballet suite *Job* and the *Sinfonia Antartica*, written in 1956 for the film *Scott of the Antarctic*.

---

[1] *New Grove*, Vol. 7, *sub nom.*

My soul doth magnify the Lord:
and my spirit hath rejoiced in God my Saviour.
For he hath regarded:
the lowliness of his hand-maiden.
For behold, from henceforth:
all generations shall call me blessed.
For he that is mighty hath magnified me:
and holy is his Name.
And his mercy is on them that fear him:
throughout all generations.
He hath shewed strength with his arm:
he hath scattered the proud in the imagination of
their hearts.
He hath put down the mighty from their seat:
and hath exalted the humble and meek.
He hath filled the hungry with good things:
and the rich he hath sent empty away.
He remembering his mercy hath holpen his servant
Israel: as he promised to our forefathers,
Abraham and his seed, for ever.

LUKE 1

PART I

Early and Medieval Hymns

The Magnificat

The song of Mary, as written down in St Luke's Gospel (1:39–56), stands at the interchange of the Jewish and Christian faiths. With its echoes of so many earlier biblical prayers and psalms, including the song of Hannah, mother of the infant prophet Samuel, the *Magnificat* is a song of praise and adoration expressed in a typical Hebrew pattern of statement and response – the power of the Lord being contrasted with the spiritual poverty of earthly rule – and, just as the mighty and rich are deposed and sent away empty, so the poor and humble are fed and their lives enriched with good things. It can be seen as a document of social democracy and liberationist principles in which Mary, whom many have identified with as an early radical thinker, well grounded in Hebraic traditions, is able to use its ancient forms to express her new relationship to God.[1]

It is this relationship that brings us into the Christian mystery. The writers of the psalms regarded themselves as insignificant in the sight of God, and his power as transcendent – a feeling expressed by the modern Israeli poet Yehuda Amichai in a radio broadcast in 1979.

> When you look [at the Judaean desert] you have a certain feeling of something far above and beyond anything which a man or a nation may ever be able to create . . . and the whole feeling of time is somehow changed . . . Perhaps this feeling in the desert is something that shaped the way our forefathers, the sons of Israel, formed their attitude towards the notion of God; and this also was at the basis that really one could no longer take a certain statue and say it's a god, because it's so small.[2]

The event to which Mary has assented – the embryonic presence of God within her – does indeed, in the Latin translation from the original Greek, 'magnify' her. We feel at once that, while she can identify on one level with the humble and meek, she takes on the mantle of the mother of God, saying quite simply that she is exalted and blessed beyond any other woman or man because she is to be the bearer of Christ into the world.

Mary speaks of this extraordinary event in an ordinary context, a domestic visit to her cousin Elizabeth, herself miraculously pregnant with John the

---

[1] Richard Harries, *A Gallery of Reflections: The Nativity of Christ* (Bible Reading Fellowship, 1995), p. 26
[2] Penelope Farmer and Jenyth Worsley, *A Jerusalem Journey* (BBC Radio 3, 1979).

Walking Madonna in Salisbury Cathedral Close, by Elizabeth Frink

Baptist. Her song has become part of one of the more domestic (though still solemn) liturgies of the Christian church, probably introduced by St Benedict for the office of Evening Prayer or Vespers, where the day is, as it were, wound down and put to rest. The *Magnificat*, in its Latin version, has been sung ever since in Gregorian and Anglican plainsong, in countless vernacular translations and in specially composed Vespers, one of the most beautiful being the setting by Claudio Monteverdi in his 1610 *Marian Vespers*, which gives full weight to the gravitas of the opening repeated 'Magnificat' from the full choir, followed by the simple line of 'anima mea Dominum', sung by a single soprano voice.

In the early 1960s, the editors of *The Anglican Hymn Book* asked Timothy Dudley-Smith (b. 1926), an evangelical priest (later bishop of Thetford) much involved with Christian mission within the Church of England, if he had any hymns for their new book. He replied that 'having no music whatsoever' he could not write hymns, but that he had written a poem, 'Tell out my soul', inspired by the first line of the *Magnificat* from a review copy of the *New English Bible*. Since then, the poem has been taken into the heart of congregations throughout the Christian communion, appearing in over twenty hymn-books. The words have been set to a variety of tunes, but Walter Greatorix's resounding *Woodlands*, first chosen by the editors of *100 Hymns for Today* (an A&M publication), expresses particularly the joyous and exultant aspect of Mary's words.

Tell out, my soul, the greatness of the Lord:
  Unnumbered blessings, give my spirit voice;
Tender to me the promise of his word;
  In God my Saviour shall my heart rejoice.

Tell out, my soul, the greatness of his name:
  Make known his might, the deeds his arm has done;
His mercy sure, from age to age the same;
  His holy name, the Lord, the Mighty One.

Tell out, my soul, the greatness of his might:
  Powers and dominions lay their glory by;
Proud hearts and stubborn wills are put to flight,
  The hungry fed, the humble lifted high.

Tell out, my soul, the glories of his word:
  Firm is his promise, and his mercy sure.
Tell out, my soul, the greatness of the Lord
  To children's children and for evermore.

From the Didache, *First Century AD*

After the *Magnificat*, our second and third hymns connect our worship today directly with the first-century experience of a small and often persecuted church. Converts needed instruction and the *Didache* (from the Greek for teaching) is now dated by scholars right back to the first century AD. So what may be our earliest surviving and complete hymn takes us back to the worship of an obscure Syrian congregation. Clement of Alexandria quotes it from the *Didache* in the second century. We owe its revival and translation to one of the modern enthusiasts for searching out ancient hymn texts, F. Bland Tucker (1895–1954). It was first published in *English Praise* (OUP, 1975, no. 62) and now appears in the NEH to a tune by Louis Bourgeois.★

Father, we thank thee who hast planted
Thy holy name within our hearts.
Knowledge and faith and life immortal
Jesus thy Son to us imparts.

Thou, Lord, didst make all for thy pleasure,
Didst give us food for all our days,
Giving in Christ the bread eternal;
Thine is the power, be thine the praise.

Watch o'er thy Church, O Lord, in mercy,
Save it from evil, guard it still,
Perfect it in thy love, unite it,
Cleansed and conformed unto thy will.

As grain, once scattered on the hillsides,
Was in this broken bread made one,
So from all lands thy Church be gathered
Into thy kingdom by thy Son.

Phos Hilaron, *Before the Fourth Century AD*

G athering secretly as dusk fell, Christians groups, a minority in a pagan culture, held an evening candle-lighting ceremony when they celebrated the eternal Light. The hymn survived in a Greek text which translates easily as 'gladsome light'. Traditionally, it was used by Christians in the catacombs of Rome. Both Keble and Bridges translated it, the latter for his *Yattendon Hymnal*. This is the version which appeared in the *EH* and now in the *NEH*. It is still part of the Orthodox church's evening liturgy and now makes a moving contribution to Western evening worship. The steadfast faith of Christians, who must often have been frightened and forlorn, shines through the darkness: 'Thee, therefore, O Most High, the world doth glorify, and shall exalt for ever.' For his *Yattendon Hymnal*, Bridges chose a tune which is associated with light in darkness: Bourgeois's★ luminous setting for the *Nunc Dimittis* from Calvin's Geneva Psalter of 1549.

NUNC DIMITTIS

O gladsome light, O grace
Of God the Father's face,
The eternal splendour wearing;
Celestial, holy, blest,
Our Saviour Jesus Christ,
Joyful in thine appearing.

Now, ere day fadeth quite,
We see the evening light,
Our wonted hymn outpouring;
Father of might unknown,
Thee, his incarnate Son,
And Holy Spirit adoring.

To thee of right belongs
All praise of holy songs,
O Son of God, Lifegiver;
Thee, therefore, O Most High,
The world doth glorify,
And shall exalt for ever.

Aurelius Clemens Prudentius
(348–c. 410)

Prudentius, a Spaniard, was born into a Roman world where a dying pagan culture was struggling to maintain its hold against a rising Christian church boosted by Constantine's dream of the Cross: 'In this sign I conquer'. In the mid–fourth century, Julian the Apostate had given new heart to the pagan cause. In the 380s, the battle centred on the altar to the god of Victory in the Roman senate house. Symmachus, *praefectus urbi* in 384 and a notable anti-Christian orator, led the fight to retain it in its old position. Eventually the pagans were defeated, largely by the efforts of Bishop Ambrose of Milan.

This was the political background to Prudentius's career. He was well educated and privileged, gaining a high place in Roman society as a lawyer and civil servant. Like Augustine, he passed through a period of loose living but suddenly, at 57, he broke with his past and retired to dedicate himself to writing Christian poetry. He was steeped in the rhythms and metres of pagan Latin poetry and now began to use these skills to write surprising, fresh-minted poetry for a new world. Helen Waddell likens it to a 'knife-edge cleaving the darkness'[1] Thus, his morning hymn (in Waddell's translation[2]) begins:

O Night and Dark	The mist sheers apart
O huddled sullen clouds	Cleft by the sun's spear.
Light enters in: the sky	Colour comes back to things
Whitens	From his bright face.
Christ comes! Depart! Depart!	

Late in life he recalled the battle with the pagans in his *Contra Symmachum*, but his most famous work was the *Psychomachia*, the battle for the Christian soul between the Virtues and Vices. This became the model for similar medieval and later dramas of spiritual conflict, and here Prudentius leads the way in psychological subtlety, for his conflict is not between repulsive ugliness and shining virtue but rather between the allure of earthly beauty and transcendent spiritual beauty.

---

[1] Helen Waddell, *The Wandering Scholars* (Constable, London, 1927, 10th reprint), p. 17.

[2] Ibid., p. 18 and Appendix A, p. 223.

This is the man who, from the fourth century, gives us a vision of the cosmic Christ in his Advent hymn *Corde natus ex parentis*: 'He is Alpha: from that Fountain all that is and has been flows; He is Omega, of all things yet to come the mystic Close ... This is he, whom seer and sybil sang in ages long gone by; this is he of old revealèd in the page of prophecy.' R. F. Davis's eloquent translation sweeps us from past history to an astonishing global vision for a still-struggling young church: 'Every tongue his name confessing, countless voices answering, evermore and evermore.'

Corde natus ex parentis

Of the Father's heart begotten,
　Ere the world from chaos rose,
He is Alpha: from that Fountain
　All that is and hath been flows;
He is Omega, of all things
　Yet to come the mystic Close,
　　Evermore and evermore.

By his word was all created;
　He commanded and 'twas done;
Earth and sky and boundless ocean,
　Universe of three in one,
All that sees the moon's soft radiance,
　All that breathes beneath the sun,

He assumed this mortal body,
　Frail and feeble, doomed to die,
That the race from dust created
　Might not perish utterly,
Which the dreadful Law had sentenced
　In the depths of hell to lie,

O how blest that wondrous birthday,
　When the Maid the curse retrieved,
Brought to birth mankind's salvation,
　By the Holy Ghost conceived;
And the Babe, the world's Redeemer,
　In her loving arms received,

This is he, whom seer and sibyl
　Sang in ages long gone by;
This is he of old revealèd
　In the page of prophecy;
Lo! he comes, the promised Saviour;
　Let the world his praises cry!

Let the storm and summer sunshine,
　Gliding stream and sounding shore,
Sea and forest, frost and zephyr,
　Day and night their Lord adore;
Let creation join to laud thee
　Through the ages evermore,

Sing, ye heights of heaven, his praises;
　Angels and Archangels, sing!
Wheresoe'er ye be, ye faithful,
　Let your joyous anthems ring,
Every tongue his name confessing,
　Countless voices answering,

Liturgy of St James

This liturgy was traditionally ascribed to St James, the brother of Jesus and first Bishop of Jerusalem. It cannot be as early as this, but was certainly in use by the mid-fifth century. It was particularly popular in the Syriac, Armenian and Georgian churches, also in Egypt and Ethiopia. A Greek version, written in the ninth century in the neighbourhood of Damascus (Vatican gr. 2282), placed a 'Cherubic Hymn' immediately after The Great Entrance.[1] Our hymn which reaches us through the translation of Gerard Moultrie (1829–85) brings to Western worshippers a characteristic theme of Eastern Orthodox worship. As the gifts of the Eucharist are prepared on earth, the heavenly host spreads its vanguard to escort the 'Light of Light' in his mystical descent, as the Cherubim and Seraphim adore him with ceaseless voice. Visually the hymn evokes the great dome paintings of Orthodox churches which represent a microcosm of the Christian universe where Christ, as 'Pantocrator', is the central focus of the cupola, and 'rank on rank the host of heaven' attend him. In such a presence, human beings can only keep silence.

The hierarchy of heaven fascinated medieval imaginations. In the early sixth century the writer known as Dionysius the Pseudo-Areopagite wrote a mystical work on the *Coelestis Hierarchia* which described the nine angelic choirs in a descending order. In a ninth-century Latin translation this attracted many leading theologians (e.g. St Thomas Aquinas and St Bonaventure in the thirteenth century). But the twelfth-century abbot, Joachim of Fiore, reversed the order in his mystical *figura* of the psaltery with ten strings, creating an ascending scale in which *Homo*, the human being, through the practice of the Seven Gifts of the Spirit and the Three Theological Virtues, rises through the hierarchy to the top tenth string: *Angeli, Archangeli, Virtutes, Potestates, Principatus, Dominationes, Throni, Cherubim, Seraphim, Homo.*[2]

---

[1] R. C. D. Jasper and G. J. Cuming, *Prayers of the Eucharist: Early and Reformed* (The Liturgical Press, Collegeville, Minnesota, N. D.), pp. 88–90.

[2] On this *figura*, see M. Reeves and B. Hirsch-Reich, *The Figurae of the Abbot Joachim of Fiore* (Clarendon Press, Oxford, 1972), pp. 202–7 & pl. 27. *Homo* here means human being.

PICARDY

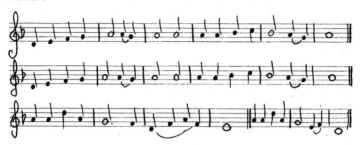

Let all mortal flesh keep silence
   And with fear and trembling stand;
Ponder nothing earthly-minded,
   For with blessing in his hand
Christ our God to earth descendeth,
   Our full homage to demand.

King of kings, yet born of Mary,
   As of old on earth he stood,
Lord of lords, in human vesture,
   In the body and the blood:
He will give to all the faithful
   His own self for heavenly food.

Rank on rank the host of heaven
   Spreads its vanguard on the way,
As the Light of light descendeth
   From the realms of endless day,
That the powers of hell may vanish
   As the darkness clears away.

At his feet the six-winged seraph;
   Cherubim with sleepless eye,
Veil their faces to the Presence,
   As with ceaseless voice they cry,
Alleluya, Alleluya,
   Alleluya, Lord most high!

Venantius Fortunatus c. 530–609

V enantius Fortunatus[1] was born at Trevisa in north Italy. He stepped into a world dominated by barbarian chieftains: Lombards, Goths, Burgundians, Franks. Yet classical culture still lived and tribal rulers aspired after it. He came to Ravenna for his education amid the jewelled glory of Byzantine mosaics. There, he said, he 'licked up a few drops of grammar and rhetoric' and lost a little of his rust on the grindstone of the law. But he nearly lost his eyesight. A drop of oil from the lamp at a shrine of St Martin restored it, and it was perhaps a desire to visit the saint's shrine at Tours that drew him north of the Alps into the land of 'seven-foot patrons'. He recorded his journeyings in eleven books of poems, many of them the charming little offerings to people he met which represented elegant culture in the midst of a harsh world. He arrived at the Frankish court of Sigebert in time to write an epithalamion for his wedding to Brunhilde of Spain. In Helen Waddell's words he 'wanders through the courts of giants a little like Gulliver'.

Clovis, the first Frankish king, had led the Franks into the Catholic church c. 503, espousing a god he deemed a great giver of victories. Savage tribal warfare mingled with acts of devout piety, especially those celebrating the church's festivals. Fortunatus was probably drawn to a deeper experience than that of his light-hearted, trifling verse when, in 567, his wanderings led him to the abbey at Poitiers where the Lady Radegunde lived. A previous Frankish king had captured her to become his reluctant queen but finally allowed her to withdraw into a life of religious austerity. Fortunatus was enchanted by her beauty, both physical and spiritual. He used his gay art to write her delicate verses. This is a snatch of one:

> O queen, that art so high
> Purple and gold thou passest by,
> With these poor flowers thy lover worships thee ...
> And when thou comest there, [to heaven]
> Hear, O my Saint, my prayer,
> And may thy kind hand draw me after thee.

---

[1] The material for this sketch is mainly drawn from H. Waddell, *The Wandering Scholars* (Constable, London, 1927, 10th edn, pp. 23–7; idem., *Medieval Latin Lyrics* (Constable, 1929), 4th edn, pp. 59–67, 300–2. All quotations are from these works.

The high occasions of the church now moved him with a mystic fervour that comes across with great power. *Vexilla regis prodeunt* ('The royal banners forward go') was written for the great processional where relics of St Martin were brought to Poitiers. It was a moment of high emotion, for the veneration of relics stirred people to their depths. Yet the metaphor of the royal banners must have evoked the image of the royal chariot, with its pagan banners, leading the tribe into battle. Fortunatus's hymn became a Crusader song.

> The royal banners forward go,
> The Cross shines forth in mystic glow,
> Where he in flesh, our flesh who made,
> Our sentence bore, our ransom paid.
>
> Where deep for us the spear was dyed,
> Life's torrent rushing from his side,
> To wash us in that precious flood,
> Where mingled water flowed, and blood.
>
> Fulfilled is all that David told
> In true prophetic song of old,
> The universal Lord is he,
> Who reigns and triumphs from the tree.
>
> O Tree of beauty, Tree of light,
> O Tree with royal purple dight,
> Elect on whose triumphal breast
> Those holy limbs should find their rest!
>
> On whose dear arms, so widely flung,
> The weight of this world's ransom hung,
> The price of humankind to pay
> And spoil the spoiler of his prey.
>
> O Cross, our one reliance, hail!
> So may thy power with us prevail
> To give new virtue to the saint,
> And pardon to the penitent.
>
> To thee, eternal Three in One,
> Let homage met by all be done:
> Whom by thy Cross thou dost restore,
> Preserve and govern evermore. Amen.

We sing both this and Fortunatus's great Passiontide hymn, *Pange lingua gloriosi proelium certaminis* ('Sing, my tongue, the glorious battle') to plainsong from the medieval *Sarum Antiphoner*. Music and words evoke another image of mysterious power – the Tree. This comes straight out of the great forests of northern Europe and belongs to the mythology of the forest peoples for whom Woden hung nine days and nine nights on the sacred tree Yggdrasill to solve the riddle of the world. For Fortunatus, as for the English poet of the *Dream of the Rood*, the Tree of the True Cross is conceived as an animate creature. It accepts its terrible destiny, as ordained by God, and becomes invested with strange glory.

> Faithful Cross! above all other,
>   One and only noble tree!
> None in foliage, none in blossom,
>   None in fruit thy peer may be;
> Sweetest wood and sweetest iron,
>   Sweetest weight is hung on thee.
>
> Sing, my tongue, the glorious battle,
>   Sing the ending of the fray,
> O'er the Cross, the victor's trophy,
>   Sound the loud triumphant lay:
> Tell how Christ, the world's Redeemer,
>   As a Victim won the day.
>
> God in pity saw man fallen,
>   Shamed and sunk in misery,
> When he fell on death by tasting
>   Fruit of the forbidden tree:
> Then another tree was chosen
>   Which the world from death should free.
>
> Bend thy boughs, O Tree of Glory,
>   Thy too rigid sinews bend;
> For awhile the ancient rigour
>   That thy birth bestowed, suspend,
> And the King of heavenly beauty
>   On thy bosom gently tend.
>
> Thou alone wast counted worthy
>   This world's Ransom to sustain,
> That a shipwrecked race might ever
>   Thus a port of refuge gain,
> With the sacred blood anointed
>   From the Lamb for sinners slain.

Venantius moves on to a bright processional hymn for Easter and Ascension, savouring all the beauties of the earth in springtime, with perhaps a lingering echo of Eostre. Here we can give only four verses of the hymn based on his Latin verse.

Salve, festa dies

Hail thee, Festival Day, blest day that art
*   hallowed for ever;*
Day wherein Christ arose, breaking the kingdom
    of death.

Lo, the fair beauty of earth, from the death of
    the winter arising,
Every good gift of the year, now with its Master
    returns.

Daily the loveliness grows, adorned with the
    glory of blossom;
Green is the woodland with leaves, bright are
    the meadows with flowers.

He who was nailed to the cross is Lord and
    the ruler of all things;
All things created on earth, worship the Maker
    of all.

St Patrick's Breastplate
and 'Be Thou My Vision'

ime-wise St Patrick (mid- or late 4th century to c. 460 or 490) is a
shadowy figure. We have no reliable date of birth and even his death
date is disputed. But the two authentic writings he left give a vivid
picture of his adventurous life: taken by pirates from his Christian home at age
16, enabled through a divine message to escape and return to Britain after six
years' slavery, called to the priesthood and finally inspired to return to Ireland
as a missionary bishop. The Ireland in which he laboured was rent by tribal
warfare, powers of darkness stalking the land in which the monasteries Patrick
established became refuges of light and gentleness. But Patrick, as the Christian
soldier, also fought the devils of blood-feud and vengeance in high places,
seeking to reconcile local chieftains and to educate their sons in more humane
ways of living.

St Patrick's Breastplate (*Lorica*), in its surviving version, dates linguistically
to the early eighth century, but it belongs to the 'genre of loricae' which surely
had its roots in an early practice of fashioning 'protective armour' by evoking
the spells of the greatest powers. So here the highest names of the Trinity, the
Incarnate Word, the Cherubim and Seraphim stand first, supported by
patriarchs, apostles, martyrs and 'all good deeds done'. But the incantation also
evokes the ancient spells of heaven and earth from 'the virtues of the star-lit
heaven' to the 'whirling wind's tempestuous shocks, the stable earth, the deep
salt sea, around the old eternal rocks'. Finally, faith returns to the whole
armour of Christ and the Trinity. In later centuries the hymn still maintained
its powers: 'Whoever shall sing it every day with pious meditation on God',
affirms the frontispiece to a manuscript in Trinity College, Dublin, 'devils will
not stay before him. It will be a safeguard to him against all poison and envy.'[1]

The version we commonly use in worship is a translation by Mrs Cecil
Frances Alexander★ (1818–95), wife of the Archbishop of Armagh and a writer
of several hymns, notably 'There is a green hill far away', which is written for
children in simple terms to explain the doctrines of the Creed.

---

[1] David Adam, *The Eye of the Eagle: Meditations on the Hymn 'Be thou my Vision'* (SPCK Triangle,
London, 1990), p. 106.

I bind unto myself today
  The strong name of the Trinity,
By invocation of the same,
  The Three in One, and One in Three.

I bind this day to me for ever,
  By power of faith, Christ's Incarnation;
His baptism in Jordan river;
  His death on cross for my salvation;
His bursting from the spicèd tomb;
  His riding up the heavenly way;
His coming at the day of doom;
  I bind unto myself today.

I bind unto myself the power
  Of the great love of Cherubim;
The sweet 'Well done' in judgement hour;
  The service of the Seraphim,
Confessors' faith, Apostles' word,
  The Patriarchs' prayers, the Prophets' scrolls,
All good deeds done unto the Lord,
  And purity of virgin souls.

I bind unto myself today
  The virtues of the star-lit heaven,
The glorious sun's life-giving ray,
  The whiteness of the moon at even,
The flashing of the lightning free,
  The whirling wind's tempestuous shocks,
The stable earth, the deep salt sea,
  Around the old eternal rocks.

I bind unto myself today
  The power of God to hold and lead,
His eye to watch, his might to stay,
  His ear to hearken to my need.
The wisdom of my God to teach,
  His hand to guide, his shield to ward;
The word of God to give me speech,
  His heavenly host to be my guard.

I bind unto myself the name,
  The strong name of the Trinity;
By invocation of the same,
  The Three in One, and One in Three.
Of whom all nature hath creation;
  Eternal Father, Spirit, Word:
Praise to the Lord of my salvation,
  Salvation is of Christ the Lord.

We catch a glimpse of Christian soldiers fighting the furies of violence in a synod of the Celtic church held at Birr (Co. Offaly) in 697, when the monk Adamnán led a determined onslaught by persuading the chieftains present to pass laws protecting women, children and non-combatants in warfare and promoting methods of reconciliation. In 1997 a commemorative celebration of this milestone event reflected its astonishing relevance to our contemporary world.

Another early Irish hymn, 'Be thou my vision', belongs to the same period. This is more introspective and intimate, reflecting the practice of many Celtic saints of withdrawing to remote and barrren places in order to make space for the presence of God. David Adam suggests that the hymn is associated with the *caim*, an early ritual in which Celtic Christians would draw a complete circle around themselves and point in the direction of the sun as a symbol of the encircling love of God.[1] But even here the background of a turbulent society is reflected in verse three, especially in its cry for the soul's shelter. Strong towers built for refuge still remain scattered over the Irish countryside, as, for instance, at the tranquil site of Clonmacnoise monastery. High kings of Ireland may have striven to impose peace on the warring clans but only the High King of Heaven could grant 'joys after vict'ry is won'.

The hymn was translated at the beginning of the twentieth century by Mary Byrne, an Anglo-Irish scholar. The version we sing, which keeps close to the original, was written by her contemporary Eleanor Hull.

SLANE

---

[1] Ibid., pp. 110–11.

Be thou my vision, O Lord of my heart,
Be all else but naught to me, save that thou art,
Be thou my best thought in the day and the night,
Both waking and sleeping, thy presence, my light.

Be thou my wisdom, be thou my true word
Be thou ever with me, and I with thee, Lord,
Be thou my great Father, and I thy true son,
Be thou in me dwelling, and I with thee one.

Be thou my breastplate, my sword for the fight,
Be thou my whole armour, be thou my true might,
Be thou my soul's shelter, be thou my strong tower,
O raise thou me heavenward, great Power of my power.

Riches I heed not, nor man's empty praise,
Be thou my inheritance now and always,
Be thou and thou only the first in my heart,
O Sovereign of heaven, my treasure thou art.

High King of heaven, thou heaven's bright Sun,
O grant me its joys after vict'ry is won,
Great Heart of my own heart, whatever befall,
Still be thou my vision, O Ruler of all.

The strong tower at Clonmachoise

St Theodulph of Orléans
(c. 750–821)

Here we meet a Visigothic Christian who fled from the Islamic advance in Spain to the court of Charlemagne at Aachen, where he was welcomed into the circle of intellectuals gathered there by the king. By 788, Theodulph was Bishop of Orléans and Abbot of Fleury. He was present in Rome at Charlemagne's coronation as emperor in 800. This Frankish court was very different in atmosphere from that in which Fortunatus had found himself. There was much exchange on theological questions. Charlemagne himself wrote a letter to his bishops asking how they understood the practice of baptism – a vital question in an age of the mass baptisms of peoples. Theodulph replied in a treatise on the double procession of the Holy Spirit. He took part in equally important discussions on the use of visual images in worship. He also made scholarly revisions of the Vulgate Bible, drawing on MSS in Spain, Italy and Gaul, and even some Hebrew sources. Following the literary fashion, he wrote 79 poems, hymns and epigrams. But, in a typical court plot in the reign of Charlemagne's son Louis the Pious, he was accused of conspiracy and exiled to Angers in 818 where he died.

His Palm Sunday processional hymn became popular throughout the Western church. It has survived for us in the Sarum liturgy (*Gloria, Laus et honor*) in which the verses are first sung by a small choir of boys and repeated by the congregation. We can picture these processions singing in plainsong Latin as they moved round a primitive abbey church or a newly built cathedral or a town church with jewelled windows and bright wall-paintings. His hymn emphasizes once again the active role of the laity in processional worship. Our modern version was translated by J. M. Neale. As a choral exercise for the whole congregation it is appropriate that the tune has been adapted from a German melody by J. S. Bach.

ST THEODULPH

All glory, laud and honour
To thee, Redeemer, King,
To whom the lips of children
Made sweet hosannas ring.

Thou art the King of Israel,
Thou David's royal Son,
Who in the Lord's name comest,
The King and blessèd One.

The company of angels
Are praising thee on high,
And mortal men and all things
Created make reply.

The people of the Hebrews
With palms before thee went;
Our praise and prayer and anthems
Before thee we present.

To thee before thy passion
They sang their hymns of praise;
To thee, now high exalted,
Our melody we raise.

Thou didst accept their praises,
Accept the prayers we bring,
Who in all good delightest,
Thou good and gracious King.

Do thou direct our footsteps
Upon our earthly way,
And bring us by thy mercy
To heaven's eternal day.

Within that blessèd City
Thy praises may we sing,
And ever raise hosannas
To our most loving King.

Rabanus Maurus (c. 776–856)

T he festivals of the church inspired many of our earliest hymns. This ancient Office Hymn was written for the feast of Pentecost. It is now attributed to Rabanus Maurus, one of the essential schoolmasters of the young church in the West. Entering the Benedictine monastery of Fulda as a child oblate, he made it a centre of Carolingian culture, writing works of grammar, chronology, biblical commentary and many others, as well as sermons and poems. Although in later life he was involved in politics as Archbishop of Mainz, his real monument is seen in his pupils, his writings and the great library he created at Fulda. Among the hymns he wrote for the monks of Fulda we may now place the *Veni, creator Spiritus,* which chimes with his global vision of the Christian faith in relation to man and nature in his *De rerum naturis* or *De universo.*

In the early seventeenth century a group of theologians, poets and other scholars who became known as the Caroline Divines were seeking to establish the true spiritual identity of Anglicanism, as between the extremes of Catholicism and Puritanism. They emphasized the life of personal spirituality, characterized by discipline, austerity, devotion and simplicity. Bishop John Cosin (1594–1672)[1] belonged to this group, as did George Herbert★. In 1627, Cosin published *A Collection of Private Devotions* in which he emphasized the observance of church festivals and ceremonies. It is natural, therefore, to find him composing an English hymn for Pentecost based on *Veni, creator Spiritus.* Cosin's style has the spare, stripped-down verse of the seventeenth century, with its unvarnished use of metaphor ('Anoint and cheer our soiléd face'). The music has come down to us in harmonized adaptations of the proper plainsong, including a simplified version by Luther. There are also several fine settings by J. S. Bach★. This is probably our most popular version of this hymn. It is still sung at major religious ceremonies, including the consecration of a Pope or bishop and the installation of a monarch, for instance Queen Elizabeth II in 1953.

---

[1] On Cosin see: *Oxford Dict. of the Christian Church, sub nom.;* Wakefield, *Dict. of Christian Spirituality, sub nom.*

VENI CREATOR

A - men.

Come, Holy Ghost, our souls inspire,
And lighten with celestial fire;
Thou the anointing Spirit art,
Who dost thy sevenfold gifts impart:

Thy blessèd unction from above
Is comfort, life, and fire of love;
Enable with perpetual light
The dullness of our blinded sight:

Anoint and cheer our soilèd face
With the abundance of thy grace:
Keep far our foes, give peace at home;
Where thou art guide no ill can come.

Teach us to know the Father, Son,
And thee, of Both, to be but One;
That through the ages all along
This may be our endless song,

Praise to thy eternal merit,
Father, Son, and Holy Spirit. Amen.

Peter Abelard (1079–1142)

Many of us associate Abelard with one of the greatest love stories of the Middle Ages, perhaps as told in Helen Waddell's novel, *Peter Abelard*.[1] In the early twelfth century he was a brilliant young academic scholar lecturing on logic and dialectics (the art of argument) to enthusiastic audiences in Paris. Much of his thinking centred on the relation of philosophy to theology: reason must be harnessed to the service of faith. Among his many works, one, entitled *Sic et Non* (Yes and No), shows how, with his razor-sharp mind, he sought to arrive at understanding the truth through setting divergent theological views against each other and resolving the conflicts. But when he applied this method in his *De Unitate et Trinitate divina*, he was accused of heresy, particularly by St Bernard★, and his views were condemned. Alongside intellectual conflicts came the personal disaster of his relationship with Heloise. Forced to leave Paris, he retired in turn to various religious houses and, at one period, to a hermitage. His bitter *Historia calamitatum mearum* (1133–6) is a rare piece of autobiography for this period. He kept in touch with Heloise and, when she became Abbess of the Convent of the Paraclete, he composed 133 hymns for her use in a personal hymn-book.[2] One of these, *O quanta qualia sunt illa sabbata* is a yearning song for the peace of the eternal sabbath after earthly turbulence is ended.

Abelard came from a feudal background and, like Bernard of Cluny glimpses a heavenly transfigured feudal court: 'What are the Monarch, his court, and his throne?' But Neale's translation loses some of the lilting rhythm of the original. Here is a verse in Monsignor Knox's free translation:

What high holiday, past our declaring,
Safe in his palace God's courtiers are sharing,
Rest after pilgrimage, spoil after fighting!
God, all in all, is their crown and requiting.

(*Westminster Hymnal*, 1940, p. 205)

---

[1] See Helen Waddell, *Peter Abelard* (Constable, London, 1933).
[2] See Routley, *Hymns*, p. 30.

O quanta qualia sunt illa sabbata

O what their joy and their glory must be,
Those endless sabbaths the blessèd ones see!
Crown for the valiant; to weary ones rest;
God shall be all, and in all ever blest.

What are the Monarch, his court, and his
    throne?
What are the peace and the joy that they own?
Tell us, ye blest ones, that in it have share,
If what ye feel ye can fully declare.

Truly Jerusalem name we that shore,
'Vision of peace,' that brings joy evermore!
Wish and fulfilment can severed be ne'er,
Nor the thing prayed for come short of the
    prayer.

We, where no trouble distraction can bring,
Safely the anthems of Sion shall sing;
While for thy grace, Lord, their voices of
    praise
Thy blessèd people shall evermore raise.

There dawns no sabbath, no sabbath is o'er,
Those sabbath-keepers have one and no more;
One and unending is that triumph-song
Which to the angels and us shall belong.

Now in the meanwhile, with hearts raised on
    high,
We for that country must yearn and must sigh,
Seeking Jerusalem, dear native land,
Through our long exile on Babylon's strand.

Low before him with our praises we fall,
Of whom, and in whom, and through whom
    are all;
Of whom, the Father; and through whom, the
    Son;
In whom, the Spirit, with these ever One.

Amen.

Bernard of Cluny (c. 1100–1150)

I t is only from his dedicatory letter to Abbot Peter the Venerable that we deduce that this Bernard was a Cluniac monk. He is known for his long poem *De contemptu mundi* from which J. M. Neale★ selected several pieces to translate as hymns. Cluny had been established in Burgundy in 909/10 as a reformed Benedictine house. Attracting many aristocratic members, it rapidly increased in size and established daughter houses in France and then further afield. The special features of its reformed rule were the increasing complexity and splendour of the daily offices, the reduction of time spent on manual labour and a new emphasis on personal devotions, which reflects the general rise of individualism in eleventh- and twelfth-century religion. The *De contemptu mundi*, as its title implies, is focused on contempt for the world, renunciation of its pleasures and warnings against its evils.

This is the background to Bernard's most famous hymn, *Urbs Sion aurea*. It expresses vividly the longing soul's contemplation of the social joys of Paradise. The main scene seems to be set in a baptized Valhalla, those halls of Sion 'conjubilant with song'. There, amidst the peace of bright pastures, the Heroes feast after their long toil in the battlefield. Their Prince is ever in their midst and the hall rings with 'the song of those that triumph, the shout of them that feast'. These yearnings for a future glory are cast in the images of a feudal society. For contrast, it is worth setting beside this medieval picture a post-Reformation vision of those redeemed by the Lamb in Isaac Watts's★ hymn 'Give me the wings of faith to rise'.

Urbs Sion aurea

Jerusalem the golden,
    With milk and honey blest,
Beneath thy contemplation
    Sink heart and voice opprest.
I know not, O I know not,
    What social joys are there,
What radiancy of glory,
    What light beyond compare.

They stand, those halls of Sion,
    Conjubilant with song,
And bright with many an angel,
    And all the martyr throng;
The Prince is ever in them,
    The daylight is serene,
The pastures of the blessèd
    Are decked in glorious sheen.

There is the throne of David,
    And there, from care released,
The song of them that triumph,
    The shout of them that feast;
And they who, with their Leader,
    Have conquered in the fight,
For ever and for ever
    Are clad in robes of white.

O sweet and blessèd country,
    Shall I ever see thy face?
O sweet and blessèd country,
    Shall I ever win thy grace?
Exult, O dust and ashes!
    The Lord shall be thy part:
His only, his for ever,
    Thou shalt be, and thou art!

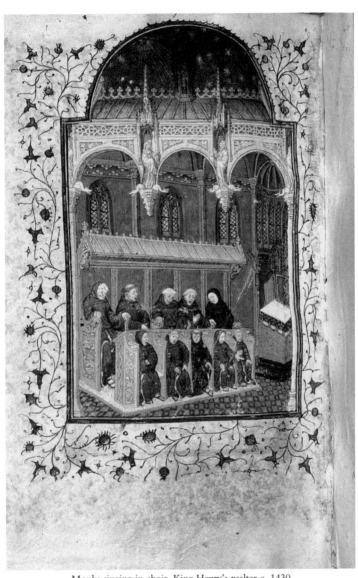

Monks singing in choir. King Henry's psalter c. 1430

Glo - ri - a, laus et ho - noc
ti - bi sit, rex Chri - ste, re - dem - ptor,
cu - i pu - e - ri - le de - cus
prom-psit ho - san - na pi - um.

Js - ra - el es tu rex
Da - vi - dis et in - clita pro - les,
no - mi - ne qui in do - mi - ni,
rex be - ne - di - cte, ve - nis.

Graduale (*Regensburg*) (see above, p. 42)

St Francis of Assisi (1182–1226)

Canticum Fratris Solis vel Laudes Creaturarum

The evidence that St Francis himself actually wrote this famous and much-loved canticle comes from the first life of the saint by his disciple Thomas of Celano, dated no later than 1228 and perhaps as early as 1220.[1] Thomas connects Francis's inspiration directly with the song of praise supposedly sung by the three young men cast into the burning fiery furnace by Nebuchadnezzar. This was inserted in the book of Daniel after chapter 2:23, but in the RV appears in the Apocrypha as the 'Song of the Three Children'. It was widely used in the church from early times and, of course, enters the *Book of Common Prayer* as the *Benedicite*.

Early stories in the *Lives* give an authentic basis for the modern image which has made Francis the patron saint of all creatures. He stands in a long tradition of saints, from the Desert Fathers to the Celtic saints of the West, who found a special affinity with creatures of all kinds.[2] Yet in affirming the goodness of God's creation, many of them, including Francis, practised a personal asceticism which belied any complacency about the powers of evil.

Our translation (by W. H. Draper, Master of the Temple) condenses the vernacular poem but follows the call to all the elements and creatures to praise very closely, as these selected stanzas from the original show:[3]

3. Laudato sie, mi signore, cun tucte le tue creature, specialmente messor lo frate sole ...
4. Et ellu è bellu e radiante cum grande splendore ...
5. Laudato si, mi signore, per sora lune e le stelle, in celu l'ai formate clarite et pretiose et belle.
6. Laudato si, mi signore, per frate vento et per aere et nubilo et sereno et omne tempo, per lo quale a le tue creature dai sustentamento.
7. Laudato si, mi signore, per sor aqua la quale è multo utile et humile et pretiosa et casta.
8. Laudato si, mi signore per frate focu per lo quale en aleumini la nocte et èllo è bello et iocundo et robustoso et forte.

---

[1] This is the view of Fr Patrick Colbourne, Ordo Minorum Capuchin (official designation of Capuchin Friars) to whom we are indebted for information and for a photocopy of the relevant section of K. Esser's book.

[2] See Helen Waddell, *Beasts and Saints* (Constable, London, 1942).

[3] From the critical edn of K. Esser, OM, *Gli Scritti di S. Francesco D'Assisi* (Padova, 1952), pp. 157–8.

9. Laudato si, mi signore, per sora nostra madre terra la quale ne sustenta et governa et produce diversi fructi con coloriti flora et herba ...
12. Laudato si, mi signore, per sora nostra morte corporale da la quale nullu homo vivente pò skappare.
14. Laudate et benedicete mi signore et rengratiate et serviate li cun grande humilitate.

> All creatures of our God and King,
> Lift up your voice and with us sing
> > Alleluya, alleluya!
> Thou burning sun with golden beam,
> Thou silver moon with softer gleam:
> > *O praise him, O praise him, Alleluya, Alleluya, Alleluya!*
>
> Thou rushing wind that art so strong,
> Ye clouds that sail in heaven along,
> > O praise him, Alleluya!
> Thou rising morn, in praise rejoice,
> Ye lights of evening, find a voice:
>
> Thou flowing water, pure and clear,
> Make music for thy Lord to hear,
> > Alleluya, Alleluya!
> Thou fire so masterful and bright,
> That givest man both warmth and light:
>
> Dear mother earth, who day by day
> Unfoldest blessings on our way,
> > O praise him, Alleluya!
> The flowers and fruits that in thee grow,
> > Let them his glory also show:
>
> And all ye men of tender heart,
> Forgiving others, take your part,
> > O sing ye, Alleluya!
> Ye who long pain and sorrow bear,
> Praise God and on him cast your care:
>
> And thou, most kind and gentle death,
> Waiting to hush our latest breath,
> > O praise him, Alleluya!
> Thou leadest home the child of God,
> And Christ our Lord the way hath trod:
>
> Let all things their Creator bless,
> And worship him in humbleness,
> > O praise him, Alleluya!
> Praise, praise the Father, praise the Son,
> > And praise the Spirit, three in One:

Thomas of Celano
(c. 13th Century)

Although not so much used now in public worship, this great medieval poem is probably known to many people from Verdi's dramatic setting in his *Requiem*. Probably originating in a late twelfth-century Benedictine prayer for the soul awaiting judgement, it became an essential part of the Mass for the Dead in the Western church.[1] The thirteenth century was swept by a wave of religious expectation and anxiety focused on the approaching Antichrist and Day of Judgement. Prophecies of the birth of the Antichrist appear scribbled in the corners of manuscripts; Roger Bacon reported horrific rumours of the tribes of Gog and Magog massing behind the Caucasus and ready to break through; Franciscans sought feverishly to fulfil Christ's last command to preach the Gospel to all the world before the imminent end. In the year 1260 – a date associated with the prophecies of Abbot Joachim – eschatological fervour mounted. Appearing first in Italy and spreading later to other countries, the explosions of the Flagellants Movement rocked communities as its participants processed from town to town flogging themselves and singing penitential psalms and *laude* (spiritual songs). This is the context in which a Franciscan, probably Thomas of Celano, transformed the original Benedictine prayer into this tremendous evocation of the Last Day when the universe would dissolve into ashes, as David and the Sibyl had prophesied, and the Last Trump would strike universal terror.

Medieval people lived in the shadow of an End to the created order which was as certain as the fact of individual death. The tremendous eight-note opening of the *Dies Irae* evokes instantaneously, in any language, the hymn's agonizing cry for mercy. The words are almost impossible to translate into English without losing the sharp thrust of the Latin.

Jeremy Irons (1812–83) provided the version in the *English Hymnal* and the *New English Hymnal*, from which we have quoted selected verses. We give below some of the original Latin verses:

---

[1] The first line, as in the thirteenth-century text, probably derives originally from the Vulgate version of Zephaniah 1:15. A Jewish hymn on the Day of Judgement, older than the *Dies Irae*, has a line which runs (in translation) 'It is a day of terror and awe.'

Dies irae, dies illa,
Solvet saeclum in favilla
Teste David cum sibylla.
Quantus tremor est futurus.
Quando iudex est venturus.
Cuncta stricte discussurus!

Tuba, mirum spargens sonum
Per sepulchra regionum
Coget omnes ante Thronum.
Rex tremendae majestatis
Qui salvandos salvas gratis
Salve me, fons pietatis.

Dies Irae

Day of wrath and doom impending,
David's word with Sybil's blending!
Heaven and earth in ashes ending!

What fear man's bosom rendeth,
When from heaven the Judge descendeth,
On whose sentence all dependeth!

Wondrous sound the trumpet flingeth,
Through earth's sepulchres it ringeth,
All before the throne it bringeth.
. . .

What shall I, frail man, be pleading?
Who for me be interceding,
When the just are mercy needing?

King of majesty tremendous,
Who dost free salvation send us,
Fount of pity, then befriend us!

Think, kind Jesu! – My salvation
Caused thy wondrous Incarnation;
Leave me not to reprobation.

Righteous Judge! for sin's pollution
Grant thy gift of absolution,
Ere that day of retribution.

Low I kneel, with heart's submission;
See, like ashes my contrition!
Help me in my last condition!

St Thomas Aquinas (c. 1227–74)

Aquinas was the intellectual giant of the thirteenth century, For him the ultimate goal of the human soul was to 'know God', and this meant primarily a union of minds; 'Contemplation,' he wrote, 'is the ascent of the mind to God through the ordinary ways of human thought, enlightened by revelation and the Holy Spirit.'[1] As a member of the Order of Preachers (Dominican), Aquinas found his teaching vocation through lectures and through his monumental expositions of the whole Christian faith, notably in the *Contra Gentiles* and his famous *Summa Theologiae*. It was natural for him to use the scholastic method of exposition which was dominant in this period in universities. Understanding came through analysis; hence he treats the great themes of theology by division, sub-division and so on, organizing argument and counter-argument in a masterly system. His works form a peak of medieval intellectual achievement.

Yet the scholastic emphasis does not give a full picture of this strange man. Physically he was a large clumsy bear of a man, the butt of monastic jokes. He was a person of great humility. Towards the end of his life he had some kind of mystic vision which led him to abandon the intellectual way, declaring that all he had written was but 'straw' compared with what he had seen. This is not so unexpected when we discover that he was known for his devotion to the daily Mass. He wrote the office for the feast of Corpus Christi.

This included an Office Hymn of appropriate objectivity and severity of form *Laud, O Sion* (NEH 521) which drives home with great authority the theology of the sacrament. Here we meet St Thomas the teacher. But a second eucharistic hymn, *Adoro te devote*, sweeps us into the mystical presence with a devotion that far transcends theological formulae. Our translation by Bishop J. R. Woodford (1820–85) conveys this well, but Gerard Manley Hopkins also made a fine translation. The *English Hymnal* sets it to a plainsong melody, but Geoffrey Webber, one-time organist at the University Church of St Mary the Virgin, Oxford, has composed an inspiring melody for it, *Radcliffe Square*.

'Loving draws us more to things than knowledge does', wrote Aquinas.[2]

---

[1] See *Oxford Dict. of the Christian Church, sub nom.*

2 Quoted Matthew Fox, *Sheer Joy Conversations with Thomas Aquinas on Creation Spirituality*. (HarperCollins, San Francisco, 1992), p. 28, from his commentary on Dionysius *De divinis nominibus*.

Thomas Aquinas

RADCLIFFE SQUARE

© Geoffrey Webber

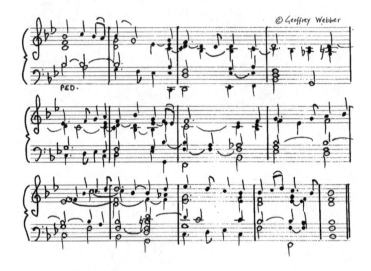

Adoro te devote

Thee we adore, O hidden Saviour, thee,
Who in thy Sacrament art pleased to be;
Both flesh and spirit in thy presence fail,
Yet here thy presence we devoutly hail.

O blest memorial of our dying Lord,
Who living bread to men doth here afford!
O may our souls for ever feed on thee,
And thou, O Christ, for ever precious be.

Fountain of goodness, Jesu, Lord and God,
Cleanse us, unclean, with thy most cleansing blood;
Increase our faith and love, that we may know
The hope and peace which from thy presence flow.

O Christ, whom now beneath a veil we see,
May what we thirst for soon our portion be,
To gaze on thee unveiled, and see thy face,
The vision of thy glory and thy grace.

The Coventry Carol

Throughout Europe, performances of the Bible stories played a part in medieval society. In the early days they were semi-staged in churches or abbeys, probably with priests and acolytes taking the speaking roles to bring home the Christmas and Easter stories to their congregations. As productions became more theatrical, the congregation moved in procession to different 'stations' or scenes set up around the church. Then, around the beginning of the thirteenth century, the churches threw open their doors to take religious drama out into the community. It was a great transformation: instead of priests and monks intoning the words in Latin, they were now spoken in a language which the audience could understand and in a form in which they could take part. These 'mystery' plays, from the French *méstier*, later *metiér*, meaning 'trade', were a great feature of the summer festival of Corpus Christi (the hymn *Pange lingua*★ was composed for a service on this day). Topics were shared out among the leading guilds or trades companies, the stories often going with the skills of a particular guild, such as the shipwrights of York who staged the tale of Noah. Leading citizens may have taken the leading roles, but there were plenty of others for good actors, including women's parts – one can imagine Mrs Noah as an early pantomime dame – while apprentices could be typecast as devils and rogues. Altogether it was an elaborate process, with written and improvised texts, actors, singers, musicians, jongleurs and comics, as well as a host of carpenters, painters, designers and costume-makers. The genre survives today in the Passion Play at Oberammergau in Bavaria, which is staged every ten years. In England, four nearly complete cycles have come down to us: from Wakefield, Chester, York and another (unknown) town.

First sung as a lullaby in a nativity pageant put on at Christmas by the company of Shearmen and Tailors in Coventry, the touching *Coventry Carol*, sung by the women of Bethlehem just before the slaughter of the Innocents by King Herod, is one of the few songs from such plays that have come down to us complete with its music. The earliest record of the pageant's performance is before Margaret of Anjou in 1456; there is a full text of the play dated twenty years earlier and the first extant version of the tune comes from a manuscript of 1591.[1]

---

[1] Erik Routley, *The English Carol* (Herbert Jenkins, London, 1958), p. 110.

Lully, lulla, thou little tiny child,
By by, lully lullay.

O sisters too,
How may we do
   For to preserve this day
This poor youngling,
For whom we do sing,
   By by, lully lullay?

Herod, the king,
In his raging,
   Chargèd he hath this day
His men of might,
In his own sight,
   All young children to slay.

That woe is me,
Poor child for thee!
   And ever morn and day,
For thy parting
Neither say nor sing
   By by, lully lullay!

Bianco of Siena (d. 1434)

Among the pious fraternities which sprang up in the fourteenth century was a Sienese group officially called the *Clerici apostolici S. Hieronymi* but popularly known as the *gesuati* because they often used ejaculatory prayers such as 'Praised be Jesus' or 'Hail Jesus'. A wealthy wool merchant, the blessed Giovanni Colombini, brought together this lay congregation about 1360 when he gave his property to a religious charity and embarked on a life of evangelical poverty and good works. Many Sienese laymen from leading families followed him and the congregation received papal approval in 1367. The members preached in many Italian cities and the order spread into southern France.[1]

The hymn which we sing in a translation by R. F. Littledale (1838–90), 'Come down, O Love divine', was written by the *gesuati* Bianco of Siena. He was a prolific composer of *laude* texts who is known to have been in Siena c. 1367 and later in Venice. It is a pentecostal hymn to the Holy Spirit and, even in translation, has a lyrical quality which must have inspired the melody of Vaughan Williams's tune, *Down Ampney*, to which it is set in *The New English Hymnal* (137).

DOWN AMPNEY

[1] Material on the *Gesuati* and Bianco is drawn from the *Dizionario biografico degli italiani*, X (1968), pp. 220–3. We acknowledge here the help of Prof. Roberto Rusconi.

Come down, O Love divine,
Seek thou this soul of mine,
And visit it with thine own ardour glowing;
O Comforter, draw near,
Within my heart appear,
And kindle it, thy holy flame bestowing.

O let it freely burn,
Till earthly passions turn
To dust and ashes in its heat consuming;
And let thy glorious light
Shine ever on my sight,
And clothe me round, the while my path illuming.

Let holy charity
Mine outward vesture be,
And lowliness become mine inner clothing;
True lowliness of heart,
Which takes the humbler part,
And o'er its own shortcomings weeps with loathing.

And so the yearning strong,
With which the soul will long,
Shall far outpass the power of human telling;
For none can guess its grace,
Till he become the place
Wherein the Holy Spirit makes his dwelling.

Preaching and singing at St Paul's Cross before James I

PART II

Sixteenth to Eighteenth Centuries

Martin Luther (1483–1546)

L uther comes over to us as an embattled warrior. Whether pictured defiantly pinning his 95 theses against indulgences to the church door at Wittenberg, or throwing an inkpot at the devil (according to legend) as he wrestled with the 'prince of hell' in the Wartburg Castle, or defying the gathered forces of the Holy Roman Empire at Worms, he was always fighting his way through. Politically, it was the rulers espousing the Lutheran cause who provided the cities of safe refuge against his many enemies. Indeed, the fate of the German Reformation was decided largely in the fortified cities. Spiritually, justifying faith was the safe stronghold which God had provided against the shafts of the devils of guilt and fear which beset Luther for most of his life.

Ein' feste burg (1528), inspired by Psalm 116, is a grand war-song of defiance. Heine called it the 'Marseillaise of the Reformation'. It almost shouts its challenge at the powers of darkness. There is no belittling the enemy: the world is full of devils waiting 'to devour us' and they may yet exact a terrible toll. But the foundations of truth in God's word are unshakeable: 'these things shall vanish all, the City of God remaineth'.

The impact of this hymn is heightened for English congregations by the fact that its translator was Thomas Carlyle, the nineteenth-century radical author. In him we see Protestantism carried to a radical extreme which makes his enthusiasm for Luther's hymn all the more understandable. He was a doughty fighter himself, and could command a tough and rugged language to match the original German. Here is the original text of verse four to compare with Carlyle's translation:

> Das Wort sie sollen lassen stahn
> und kein'Dank dazu haben;
> er ist bei uns wohl auf dem Plan
> mit seinem Geist und Gaben.
> Nehmen sie den Leib,
> Gut, Ehr, Kind und Weib:
> lass fahren dahin,
> sie habens kein' Gewinn,
> das Reich muss uns doch bleiben.

The tune was written by Luther himself and harmonized by J. S. Bach. Its strong steady beat carries with it the weight of the words and the triumphant major key has no hint of doubts or uncertainty in God's protection for the saved.

A safe stronghold our God is still,
    A trusty shield and weapon;
He'll help us clear from all the ill
    That hath us now o'ertaken.
        The ancient prince of hell
        Hath risen with purpose fell;
        Strong mail of craft and power
        He weareth in this hour;
    On earth is not his fellow.

With force of arms we nothing can,
    Full soon were we down-ridden;
But for us fights the proper Man,
    Whom God himself hath bidden.
        Ask ye, Who is this same?
        Christ Jesus is his name,
        The Lord Sabaoth's Son;
        He, and no other one,
    Shall conquer in the battle.

And were this world all devils o'er
    And watching to devour us,
We lay it not to heart so sore;
    Not they can overpower us.
        And let the prince of ill
        Look grim as e'er he will,
        He harms us not a whit;
        For why? – his doom is writ;
    A word shall quickly slay him.

God's word, for all their craft and force,
    One moment will not linger,
But, spite of hell, shall have its course;
    'Tis written by his finger.
        And though they take our life,
        Goods, honour, children, wife,
        Yet is their profit small;
        These things shall vanish all,
    The city of God remaineth.

William Kethe (d. 1594)

William Kethe was one of a group of Protestant English and Scottish divines who fled to Geneva in the mid-1550s to escape the persecutions of Mary Tudor during the course of her reign (1553–8). When it was safe to return, Kethe settled in Dorset, where he remained rector of Childe Okeford until his death, 40 years after his most famous work had been written in Geneva.

One can hardly exaggerate the importance as a catalyst for the Christian faith of this small city-state and its most noted citizen, the theologian John Calvin. Passing through Geneva in 1531, during a period of exile from France, Calvin was persuaded to remain there and set up a reformed Protestant church. By 1541, the Calvinists had established political as well as religious authority in a theocratic regime that ordered its citizens' social life and their religious worship, outlawing the so-called frivolous pastimes of instrumental music, dancing and games. One of Calvin's first acts was to arrange for the Psalms to be translated into French. For the *Geneva Psalter* he commissioned 49 texts from the poet Clément Marot and music from the Huguenot composer Louis Bourgeois★, who wrote or arranged some 39 tunes. Calvin's own translations were considered models in style: lucid, concise and austere.

The Marian exiles who arrived in Geneva were deeply influenced by Calvin's reforms. The Scots, led by John Knox, took home not only the nucleus of a new psalter but a firm commitment to a Calvinistic way of life. The English, among them John Hopkins, William Kethe, Thomas Norton and William Whittingham, were concerned with a new translation of the Bible (the Geneva or 'Breeches' Bible) and they also compiled a *Forme of Prayers* with metrical psalms attached. This Anglo-Genevan psalter of 1556 included several Genevan-psalter tunes by Bourgeois which we still sing. The book became the basis for the first complete English psalter (Sternhold and Hopkins, 1562).

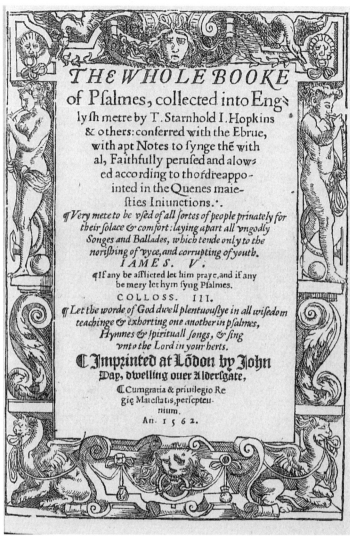

THE WHOLE BOOKE

of Pſalmes, collected into Eng∫
ly∫h metre by T.Starnhold I.Hopkins
& others:conferred with the Ebrue,
with apt Notes to ſynge thē with
al, Faithfully peruſed and alow∫
ed according to thoſdreappo-
inted in the Quenes maie-
ſties Iniunctions.∴.

¶ Very mete to be vſed of all ſortes of people priuately for
their ſolace & comfort: laying apart all vngodly
Songes and Ballades, which tende only to the
nori∫hing of vyce, and corrupting of youth.

IAMES. V.

¶ If any be afflicted let him praye,and if any
be mery let hym ſyng Pſalmes.

COLLOSS. III.

¶ Let the worde of God dwell plentuou∫lye in all wiſedom
teachinge & exhorting one another in pſalmes,
Hymnes & ſpirituall ſongs, & ſing
vnto the Lord in your herts.

**¶ Imprinted at Lōdon by John
Day, dwelling ouer Aldersgate,**

¶ Cum gratia & priuilegio Re
giē Maieſtatis,perſepteu-
nium.

An. 1 5 6 2.

Title page of Sternhold & Hopkins *Whole book of Psalmes*

Kethe's metrical version of Psalm 100 has a clarity and simplicity which makes it one of the few from this period that has survived in our hymn-books. He follows the pattern of the original Hebrew, where each verse consists of two parts in parallel that balance or answer each other. Thus Coverdale's translation for the psalm: 'O be joyful in the Lord, all ye lands: Serve the Lord with gladness: come before his presence with a song', becomes in Kethe's words: 'All people that on earth do dwell, sing to the Lord with cheerful voice.'

This is one of the very few early metrical psalms written in long rather than common metre – a choice which gives added weight to the words. The melody came from Geneva, but probably originated in an Antwerp psalter of 1539. It is now known as *The Old Hundredth*, but this was a later title to indicate that the tune originated in the old version of the psalms (i.e. Sternhold and Hopkins) rather than the New Version (i.e. Tate and Brady). It is interesting to note that Tate and Brady used the same tune in 1692, calling it *Savoy*, for a different and weaker translation of Psalm 100 than Kethe's, and Kethe's not Tate's words have survived.

OLD HUNDREDTH

A - men.

All people that on earth do dwell,
    Sing to the Lord with cheerful voice;
Him serve with fear, his praise forth tell,
    Come ye before him, and rejoice.

The Lord, ye know, is God indeed,
    Without our aid he did us make;
We are his folk, he doth us feed,
    And for his sheep he doth us take.

O enter then his gates with praise,
    Approach with joy his courts unto;
Praise, laud, and bless his name always,
    For it is seemly so to do.

For why? the Lord our God is good:
    His mercy is for ever sure;
His truth at all times firmly stood,
    And shall from age to age endure.

To Father, Son, and Holy Ghost,
    The God whom heaven and earth adore,
From men and from the Angel-host
    Be praise and glory evermore.   Amen.

Edmund Spenser (c. 1552–99)

The essence of Elizabethan romantic chivalry seems to be concentrated in this young poet, one of whose closest friends was Sir Philip Sidney, the model 'perfect courtier'. Born in London, his headmaster at the newly founded Merchant Taylor's School was the Liberal, Mulcaster, well known for his generous idea of education: 'It is not a mind, nor a body that we have to educate', he said 'but a man; and we cannot divide him.'[1] So young Edmund was educated in Greek and Latin classical studies, music and drama. His first appearance before the Queen was probably as a boy actor in one of the plays which Mulcaster yearly presented at Court. He published his first essay in poetry as a schoolboy. From 1569 to 1576 he studied at Cambridge where he fell deeply under the spell of the prevailing Platonic idealism which he sought to translate into poetry.

But to give his life to poetry he needed patrons. His introduction to the Earl of Leicester and, through him, to Sidney, was a first step of good fortune. He accepted Sidney's serious commitment to the Protestant cause but in both these friends Puritanism was deeply tinged with Platonic mysticism, while both set themselves to adapt to modern life the ideals of medieval chivalry. Preferment finally came in 1580 when he was appointed private secretary to Lord Grey, the new Lord Deputy of Ireland. He spent a large part of his remaining life in Ireland where his official duties left him time to write his greatest poem, *The Faerie Queene*, and various other works.

Spenser's vision of heroic adventure and the idealized society of the new age find their highest expression in this long romantic poem dedicated to Elizabeth, especially in the opening legend of the Red Cross Knight or the Knight of Holiness, whose experiences, in a strange way, parallel those of Bunyan's★ Pilgrim, though in a very different mode. The theme of idealized love in its many aspects is explored in the long series of 89 sonnets, the *Amoretti*.[2] In 1594 he married Elizabeth Boyle and dedicated this sequence to her, with an epithalamion to celebrate their wedding. It is in the *Amoretti*, in Sonnet 68, that he sublimes his pursuit of love and beauty in our hymn

---

[1] Edmund Spenser, *The Poetical Works of Edmund Spenser* (with an Introduction by E. de Selincourt) (OUP, 1916), Introduction, p. viii.
[2] Ibid., pp. 561–78.

'Most glorious Lord of Lyfe'.[1] Its Protestant theology of salvation through the blood of Christ is explicitly stated, but the hymn rises to a rare spiritual ecstasy in the sheer joy of devotion poured out.

Henry Lawes's stately tune begins every line with a long note, called colloquially a 'gathering note'. This was a kindly and useful device whereby the choir stayed on the first note long enough for the congregation to join in, rather than come in later and miss the start of the hymn.

FARLEY CASTLE

> Most glorious Lord of life, that on this day
>   Didst make thy triumph over death and sin,
> And having harrowed hell, didst bring away
>   Captivity thence captive, us to win:
>
> This joyous day, dear Lord, with joy begin,
>   And grant that we for whom thou diddest die,
> Being with thy dear blood clean washed from
>   sin,
>   May live for ever in felicity:
>
> And that thy love we weighing worthily,
>   May likewise love thee for the same again;
> And for thy sake, that all like dear didst buy,
>   With love may one another entertain;
>
> So let us love, dear Love, like as we ought;
> Love is the lesson which the Lord us taught.

---

[1] Ibid., p. 573.

Pastor Philipp Nicholai
(1556–1608)

W hat may well be judged our grandest Advent hymn was conceived under strange circumstances.[1] Philipp Nicolai was the Lutheran pastor in the Westphalian town of Unna when, in 1597, it was stricken by a terrible visitation of the plague. In a short time around 1300 townspeople died. He sought to bring comfort to his flock by pointing steadfastly to the coming of Christ in glory. Whatever early disaster befalls us, he said, it is never an end but the beginning of a more glorious future.

Our hymn was composed within a work of meditation entitled *A Mirror of Joy*. It at once evokes two solemn images: the watchmen who sing when the Lord returns to Zion, from Isaiah 52:8 in the Old Testament, and the joy of the wise virgins when they greet the bridegroom at the marriage feast, from Matthew 25:1–13 in the New Testament.

Nicolai also composed the tune which was harmonized by J. S. Bach. There are several English translations, including one by Catherine Winkworth; all use the same metre and tune. Frances Burkitt (1864–1935) has given us a free but thrilling translation, full of urgency and splendour. Yet the tune takes us at a deliberate, majestic pace: the Advents of Christ are unhurried but certain.

WACHET AUF

---

[1] See Routley, *Hymns*, p. 41, for the background to this hymn.

Wake, O wake! with tidings thrilling
The watchmen all the air are filling,
    Arise, Jerusalem, arise!
Midnight strikes! no more delaying,
'The hour has come!' we hear them saying.
        Where are ye all, ye virgins wise?
            The Bridegroom comes in sight,
            Raise high your torches bright!
                Alleluya!
            The wedding song
            Swells loud and strong:
    Go forth and join the festal throng.

Sion hears the watchmen shouting,
Her heart leaps up with joy undoubting,
    She stands and waits with eager eyes;
See her Friend from heaven descending,
Adorned with truth and grace unending!
        Her light burns clear, her star doth rise.
            Now come, thou precious Crown,
            Lord Jesu, God's own Son!
                Hosanna!
            Let us prepare
            To follow there,
        Where in thy supper we may share.

Every soul in thee rejoices;
From men and from angelic voices
    Be glory given to thee alone!
Now the gates of pearl receive us,
Thy presence never more shall leave us,
        We stand with Angels round thy throne.
            Earth cannot give below
            The bliss thou dost bestow.
                Alleluya!
            Grant us to raise,
            To length of days,
        The triumph-chorus of thy praise.

Martin Rinkart (1586–1649)

T he opening word 'Now' (*Nun* in the original) gives a sense of crisis resolved, of finality reached, to this great outburst of gratitude, reflecting the political context out of which it was born. Martin Rinkart was the pastor of his home village Eilenberg during the terrible days of the Thirty Years War in Germany, when the apocalyptic horsemen of plague and famine rode the countryside in the wake of ravaging armies. Plague reached Eilenburg in 1637 and in the midst of its sufferings the occupying Swedish army demanded tribute of 30,000 thalers. Rinkart prayed desperately to God, but he also negotiated and got the levy reduced to 2000 thalers.[1] It seems fitting to date the hymn to this moment. Its message would be that, while human enterprise can help, our ultimate refuge and strength is in God. In fact, this hymn may have been written earlier. Whatever its date it was certainly widely used for thanksgiving when, in 1648, the Treaty of Westphalia ended this suicidal conflict.

As in Germany, so in England, *Nun danket* has become a thanksgiving for great occasions since it was brought to us in 1858 by that doughty translator of German hymns, Catherine Winkworth★. The tune, *Nun danket*, has been ascribed to Johann Crüger, a contemporary cantor at St Nicholas Church, Berlin, but it may have been written by Rinkart himself.

---

[1] Routley, *Hymns*, p. 43.

NUN DANKET

Now thank we all our God,
With heart and hands and voices,
  Who wondrous things hath done,
In whom his world rejoices;
  Who from our mother's arms
    Hath blessed us on our way
With countless gifts of love,
  And still is ours to-day.

O may this bounteous God
Through all our life be near us,
  With ever joyful hearts
And blessèd peace to cheer us;
  And keep us in his grace,
    And guide us when perplexed,
And free us from all ills
  In this world and the next.

All praise and thanks to God
The Father now be given,
  The Son, and him who reigns
With them in highest heaven,
  The One eternal God,
    Whom earth and heaven adore;
For thus it was, is now,
  And shall be evermore.   Amen.

George Herbert (1593–1633)

I t is fitting that the sculpture of the priest–poet George Herbert at Edington Church, in Wiltshire, should be holding a lute, for it is both a symbol of his poetic art and also of the taut agony of Christ on the Cross, as expressed in his poem *Easter*:

> Awake my lute, and struggle for thy part
> > With all thy art.
> The crosse taught all wood to resound his name
> > Who bore the same,
> His stretched sinews taught all strings what key
> Is best to celebrate this most high day.

Salisbury on Herbert was born into a family accustomed to position and patronage. His mother, Magdalen Herbert, was patron and friend of the poet John Donne, while her son Edward was given a peerage after a career as soldier and diplomat. At first this young man from the Welsh Marches followed a traditional path; elected a fellow of Trinity College, Cambridge, and obtaining the prestigious post of public orator. The post was important to any man of ambition as it gave him an entrée to the court of James I in London. From 1624 to 1625 Herbert was one of the king's men in Parliament, as member for the Welsh constituency of Montgomery. At this time, in his twenties, his first biographer, Izaak Walton, described him as someone who 'always addressed his inferiors from a very great distance'.[1] But Herbert's circle included Donne and Nicholas Ferrar, a Cambridge contemporary who encouraged him to study divinity, and who later set up a religious community for Anglicans in Little Gidding, based on the principles of private devotion, study and charitable works. It is likely that Herbert may have stayed there; at any rate, some kind of conversion seems to have happened. Certainly the sensitive and introspective face that looks at us from the church sculpture is not that of a man pursuing 'court hopes'. As his fellowship required, he was ordained deacon around 1624. Five years later he was installed as rector in Bemerton, just south of Salisbury, where he became known as a man of meditation, humility and charitable works – also one who had the energy to care for his parishioners, preach sermons not exceeding an hour in length, and walk to

---

[1] Moelwyn Merchant, *George Herbert* (Friends of Edington, Westbury, 1984).

Salisbury on Thursdays with his lute on his back for evensong in the cathedral, followed by an evening of music-making. As well as poetry and sermons, he was writing a delightful handbook for country parsons, *A Priest to the Temple or the Country Parson*, which advised on such matters as preaching skills and the use of 'colours and light' as an aid to worship.

Let all the world in every corner sing,
    My God and King!
  The heavens are not too high,
His praise may thither fly;
  The earth is not too low,
  His praises there may grow.
Let all the world in every corner sing,
    My God and King!

Let all the world in every corner sing,
    My God and King!
  The Church with psalms must shout,
  No door can keep them out;
  But above all, the heart
  Must bear the longest part.
Let all the world in every corner sing,
    My God and King!

Some of Herbert's best-known poems have come down to us as hymns chosen by John Wesley for inclusion in his 1737 hymn-book, though they are now sung to nineteenth-century tunes. They had first appeared a century earlier, in 1633, in a collection entitled *The Temple*, which he had sent to Nicholas Ferrar when he knew he was dying. Many were composed after a morning's meditation on a religious text and were, he wrote, 'a picture of the many spiritual conflicts that have passed betwixt God and my soul'.

Contemporary critics of Herbert and Donne called such verse 'strong-lined' – not intended as praise (the term 'metaphysical poets' was invented later as a pejorative term by Dr Samuel Johnson). Their poetry can be irregular in form, anti-romantic, personal, often with unlikely comparisons or conceits and abrupt opening lines which take the reader straight into the middle of a scene or a conversation. Both bring to their religious poetry a sense of the actual and ordinary drawn from non-religious experience. So, in the poem *Praise* ('King of glory, King of peace') we have a simple metaphor of the countryside, 'And the cream of all my heart I will bring thee'.

GWALCHMAI

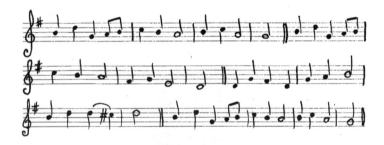

King of glory, King of peace,
  I will love thee;
And that love may never cease,
  I will move thee.
Thou hast granted my request,
  Thou hast heard me;
Thou didst note my working breast,
  Thou hast spared me.

Wherefore with my utmost art
  I will sing thee,
And the cream of all my heart
  I will bring thee.
Though my sins against me cried,
  Thou didst clear me;
And alone, when they replied,
  Thou didst hear me.

Seven whole days, not one in seven,
  I will praise thee;
In my heart, though not in heaven,
  I can raise thee.
Small it is, in this poor sort
  To enrol thee:
E'en eternity's too short
  To extol thee.

In the second verse of *The Elixir* ('Teach me, my God and King') the experience of seeing God's creation is likened to someone looking out of the window: the eye can stop at the glass, or it can look through and see the heavens beyond. The last verse points up this conceit: the philosopher's stone, which alchemists have sought in vain, is, in fact, available for anyone who is able to change their focus on life, and the 'Elixir' of the title is the eucharistic wine which enables this transformation to be made.

SANDYS

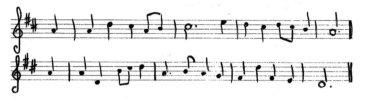

Teach me, my God and King,
In all things thee to see;
And what I do in anything
To do it as for thee!

A man that looks on glass,
On it may stay his eye;
Or if he pleaseth, through it pass,
And then the heaven espy.

All may of thee partake;
Nothing can be so mean,
Which with this tincture, 'for thy sake',
Will not grow bright and clean.

A servant with this clause
Makes drudgery divine;
Who sweeps a room, as for thy laws,
Makes that and the action fine.

This is the famous stone
That turneth all to gold;
For that which God doth touch and own
Cannot for less be told.

Paul Gerhardt (1607–76)

Inextricably connected with Good Friday worship is the mourning hymn which Paul Gerhardt translated from the last part of a late medieval Latin poem. By the eighteenth century it had already been translated into English and, in 1861, Sir Henry Baker made another translation for *Hymns Ancient and Modern*. But the version generally used now is that which Robert Bridges★ made for his *Yattendon Hymnal*★. Although Bridges went back to the Latin original, his words still seem to catch the essence of Lutheran spirituality in its controlled emotion, perhaps because it is universally sung to J. S. Bach's 'Passion Chorale'. But this itself has a strange origin: the melody was composed originally by Hans Leo Hassler (1564–1612) for a love-song. Bach, of course, used it several times.

PASSION CHORALE

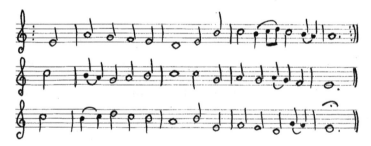

O sacred head, sore wounded,
    Defiled and put to scorn;
O kingly head, surrounded
    With mocking crown of thorn:
What sorrow mars thy grandeur?
    Can death thy bloom deflower?
O countenance whose splendour
    The hosts of heaven adore.

Thy beauty, long-desirèd,
    Hath vanished from our sight;
Thy power is all expirèd,
    And quenched the light of light.
Ah me for whom thou diest,
    Hide not so far thy grace:
Show me, O Love most highest,
    The brightness of thy face.

I pray thee, Jesus, own me,
    Me, Shepherd good, for thine;
Who to thy fold hast won me,
    And fed with truth divine.
Me guilty, me refuse not,
    Incline thy face to me,
This comfort that I lose not,
    On earth to comfort thee.

In thy most bitter passion
    My heart to share doth cry,
With thee for my salvation
    Upon the Cross to die.
Ah, keep my heart thus movèd
    To stand thy Cross beneath,
To mourn thee, well-belovèd,
    Yet thank thee for thy death.

My days are few, O fail not,
    With thine immortal power,
To hold me that I quail not
    In death's most fearful hour:
That I may fight befriended,
    And see in my last strife
To me thine arms extended
    Upon the Cross of life.

Gerhardt, like other German hymn-writers, was a Lutheran pastor. He wrote over a 100 hymns, including our second selected one which takes us into a completely different mood, evoking an evening meditation under a starlit sky. Human frailty is transcended and embraced by the Creator's love. In these two contrasting hymns, Bridges's sensitivity as a translator is seen at its best.

INNSBRUCK

The duteous day now closeth,
Each flower and tree reposeth,
  Shade creeps o'er wild and wood:
Let us, as night is falling,
On God our Maker calling,
  Give thanks to him, the Giver good.

Now all the heavenly splendour
Breaks forth in starlight tender
  From myriad worlds unknown;
And man, the marvel seeing,
Forgets his selfish being,
  For joy of beauty not his own.

His care he drowneth yonder,
Lost in the abyss of wonder;
  To heaven his soul doth steal:
This life he disesteemeth,
The day it is that dreameth,
  That doth from truth his vision seal.

Awhile his mortal blindness
May miss God's loving kindness,
  And grope in faithless strife:
But when life's day is over
Shall death's fair night discover
  The fields of everlasting life.

John Milton (1608–74)

In Milton we see diverse currents of thought and politics, which swept through the seventeenth century, contending with each other. His literary education at St Paul's School and Christ's College, Cambridge, carried him into the late Renaissance classical culture which finds expression in his early poems *L'Allegro* and *Il Penseroso*, and in the masque of *Comus*. At Cambridge, too, he came under the liberal influence of the Cambridge Platonists.[1] He thought of taking holy orders but abandoned the idea as, increasingly, he perceived the 'tyranny' of Archbishop Laud's regime. Puritan radicalism was now pressing in on him and, in 1641, he joined the Presbyterian cause. From this time, his writings become increasingly polemical and political, notably in attacks on prelacy and defence of freedom of the press (see his famous *Areopagitica*). As the political crisis came to a head he moved towards Independency. He supported Cromwell and the Commonwealth but championed the freedom of religious sects. When the Restoration destroyed his political hopes he returned to his literary vocation, now dedicated to the high theological matter of *Paradise Lost* (1665) and *Paradise Regained* (1671). In a period of clashing orthodoxies, Milton pursued a completely individual line: his theological views were often unconventional; in politics he stood for both order and freedom of mind, while his literary genius often clothed Puritan religious sentiment in the conceits and language of the contemporary humanist culture.

Milton did not write hymns, but he composed translations and paraphrases of psalms in a variety of poetic forms, including the type of metrical verse used in Puritan worship. The 1645 edition of his *Minor Poems* states that Psalm 136 and the preceding one 'was don by the author at fifteen years old'. Some of the stanzas reciting the early history of Israel show a schoolboy's relish for vivid imagery and proper names. Here are some of the verses omitted in the hymn:

> He with his thunder-clasping hand
> Smote the first born of Egypt's land ...
>
> The ruddy waves he cleft in twain
> Of the Erythràean main ...
>
> And large-limb'd Ogg he did subdue
> With all his over-hardy crew ...[2]

---

[1] On the Cambridge Platonists, see *Oxford Dict. of the Christian Church, sub nom.*

[2] Psalm CXXXVI, verses 10, 12, 18 in any edition of Milton's poems.

The full text of 24 verses has been judiciously edited as a hymn but the version we sing has a simplicity of expression which Milton had moved away from by his twenties[1] – he was by then writing verse fluently in Latin and Italian. It is illuminating to compare it with one of his religious poems, the 'Ode on the Morning of Christ's Nativity' (1629). Here the Christchild is 'the mighty Pan', the angels' song is the music of the spheres, while Apollo and all the ancient gods are dethroned in a series of elaborate images. By contrast, our hymn is more severe. It keeps close to the original, using at the end of every verse the refrain from the psalm itself: 'For his mercy endureth for ever'. Even here, however, he easily incorporates the poetic images of the 'golden-tressèd sun', the 'hornèd moon' and others.

The tune by Jon Antes was imported (by John Wesley) from a collection compiled by the German theologian Johann Freylinghausen; Wesley's copy of his *Gesangbuch* is still in existence.

> Let us, with a gladsome mind,
> Praise the Lord, for he is kind:
> *For his mercies ay endure,*
> *Ever faithful, ever sure.*
>
> Let us blaze his name abroad,
> For of gods he is the God:
>
> He with all-commanding might
> Filled the new-made world with light:
>
> He the golden-tressèd sun
> Caused all day his course to run:
>
> And the hornèd moon by night,
> Mid her spangled sisters bright:
>
> All things living he doth feed,
> His full hand supplies their need:
>
> Let us with a gladsome mind,
> Praise the Lord for he is kind:

---

[1] Later Milton paraphrased further psalms, including Psalms 82, 85 and 86 from which selected verses form our hymn 'The Lord will come and not be slow' (NEH 15). See Introduction, n. 20.

Richard Baxter (1615–1691)

I t is something of a miracle to meet in the middle of conflict-ridden seventeenth-century England a character as eirenic as Baxter. At a time of bitter dogmatic divisions he argued for a catholic inclusiveness, saying 'God hath not made our Judgements all of one complexion no more than our faces'.[1] He tried to redirect religious passions from rival creeds and liturgies to the practise of a sincere devotional piety. This he called 'catholic' or 'mere' Christianity (a term later adopted by C.S. Lewis).[2]

Baxter came from a Shropshire background. The patronage of Sir Henry Herbert took him to London but he became disgusted at the Court frivolity and, at the same time, was greatly influenced by two nonconformist ministers. Ordained in the Anglican Church, he discovered his gift as a pastor, to hand-loom weavers in particular, and worked for co-operation between episcopal and nonconformist clergy in the common pastoral task. As conflicting ideologies hardened in the Cromwellian period, he increasingly became the champion of moderation. At the Restoration he worked for a comprehensive settlement and was therefore deeply disappointed by the Act of Uniformity. His doubts about episcopacy came to a head when he declined the bishopric of Hereford, reluctantly withdrawing from the Church of England to become a leader of the moderate Presbyterians. In this role he suffered persecution but lived to accept the Act of Toleration (1689).

Throughout his troubled life Baxter seems to have been sustained by a deep sense of joy in the goodness of God. Unusually for a Puritan theologian he found the road to heavenly contemplation through delight in natural beauty, in music and in the enjoyment of the senses generally. A chapter in his *Saints' Everlasting Rest*, first published in 1650, is headed: 'Heavenly contemplation assisted by Sensible Objects'.[3] He writes:

> To rejoice in what we never saw ... is not so easy as to rejoice in what we see and possess. It must therefore be a point of spiritual prudence to call in sense to the assistance of faith. It will be a good work if we can make friends of these usual enemies and make them instruments for raising us to God ... Think with thyself, 'How sweet is food to my taste ... How delightful are grateful odours to the

---

[1] Quoted Wakefield, *Dict. of Christian Spirituality*, *sub nom.*
[2] Ibid.

smell! or music to the ear! or beautiful sights to the eye! ... Compare also the delights above with those we find in natural knowledge ... What exquisite pleasure is it to dive into the secrets of nature ... What sweetness is there in the exercise of natural love, whether to children, parents, yoke fellows or intimate friends!... How does the majesty of the Creator shine in the fabric of this world! These and many more earthly delights are but pointers: What delights are there, then, at God's right hand, where we shall know in a moment all that is to be known.[1]

In the hymn selected here, heavenly joy streams down through the hierarchy of the universe, from the celestial realm to the single soul. Against the background of the turbulent times in which he lived, this hymn carries a particular poignancy, especially in the last verse even though this was not actually written by him: 'Let all thy days till life shall end whate'er he send be filled with praise.' The version of this hymn which we now sing is an adaptation by J. H. Gurney (1802–62).

Ye holy angels bright,
   Who wait at God's right hand,
Or through the realms of light
   Fly at your Lord's command,
     Assist our song,
       For else the theme
       too high doth seem
     For mortal tongue.

Ye blessèd souls at rest,
   Who ran this earthly race
And now, from sin released,
   Behold the Saviour's face,
     God's praises sound,
       As in his sight
       With sweet delight
     Ye do abound.

Ye saints, who toil below,
   Adore your heavenly King,
And onward as ye go
   Some joyful anthem sing;
     Take what he gives
       And praise him still,
       Through good or ill,
     Who ever lives!

My soul bear thou thy part,
   Triumph in God above:
And with a well-tuned heart
   Sing thou the songs of love!
     Let all thy days
       Till life shall end
       what e'er he send
     Be filled with praise.

---

[1] R. Baxter, *The Saints Everlasting Rest: or A Treatise of the Blessed State of the Saints in their Enjoyment of God in Heaven* (The Religious Tract Society, London, n.d.), pp. 315–21.

John Bunyan (1628–1688)

B
unyan is the epitome of the pilgrim: his hymn can be sung with fervour today by many types of 'searcher'. Like Luther, though his background was so different, he was tormented from youth by feelings of guilt and insecurity. A turbulent soul in a turbulent society, he was caught in what he believed to be the cosmic conflict between God and the Devil. In his autobiography, *Grace Abounding to the Chief of Sinners* (pub. 1666) he describes vividly how, as a foul-mouthed tinker, he took his fill of sin, 'playing the Madman' and going on in sin 'with great greediness of mind',[1] yet never satisfied. Envying the happiness of some poor women sitting in the sun at Bedford and talking about the things of God, he had a vision in which, as it were, they sat on the sunny side of a high mountain while he shivered outside the wall set between them.[2] After a huge effort he squeezed through a tiny gap to join them. This signified the half-conversion of a reformed life, but the Tempter continued to assault him with gnawing doubts that he could be saved through his own efforts, only by the grace he could not find: 'I blessed the condition of the Dogge and Toad and counted the estate of everything God had made far better than this dreadful state of mine'.[3] But after a time of great darkness, 'as I was sitting by the fire I suddenly felt this word to sound in my heart *I must go to Jesus*; at this my former darkness and atheism fled away and the blessed things of heaven were set within my view'. He was inwardly directed in mind to Hebrews 12:22–4: 'Ye are come to mount Sion ... to an innumerable company ... to Jesus the Mediator' ... 'Then with joy I told my wife, O now I know, I know ...'[4] In 1655 he joined the Baptist Church at Bedford and became an itinerant preacher.

At the Restoration he was imprisoned for holding unlawful meetings and, in all, spent more than twelve years in Bedford Gaol. Ironically, this gave him a far wider influence than his preaching would ever have done, for his literary genius was enabled to pour itself into writings, of which *The Pilgrim's Progress* was the chief. His education had been rudimentary: he himself says that he had not 'borrowed my doctrine from Libraries'; 'I never went to school to Aristotle

---

[1] *Grace Abounding to the Chief of Sinners*, ed. R. Sharrock (Clarendon Press, Oxford, 1962), p. 11.
[2] Ibid., pp. 19–20.
[3] Ibid., p. 33.
[4] Ibid., p. 82.

Christian loses his Burden at the Cross

or Plato' or knew 'the Mode nor Figure of a syllogism'. His vivid characterizations and trenchant phrases rose straight from a well of intense personal experience. Here the countryside is that of Bedfordshire but the pilgrimage is that of Everyman, providing us with many metaphors of our common life: the Slough of Despond, the pilgrim's burden, the Hill Difficulty (with its seductive arbour for sleeping halfway up), Giant Despair's Castle, Vanity Fair, the fight with Apollyon in the Valley of Humiliation, the Delectable Mountains, the Celestial City.

The two poems selected here are songs from part 2 (pub. 1684) of *The Pilgrim's Progress*. This recounts the pilgrimage of Christiana and her children following Christian, her husband. Mr Greatheart leads them and, as they go through the Valley of Humiliation where Christian had been so beset, they meet a shepherd boy singing to himself the song of contentment. Says Greatheart: 'I dare say this boy leads a merrier life than he that is clad in silk and velvet.'[1]

> He that is down, need fear no fall;
> He that is low, no pride;
> He that is humble ever shall
> Have God to be his guide.
>
> I am content with what I have,
> Little be it or much;
> And, Lord, contentment still I crave,
> Because thou savest such.
>
> Fulness to such a burden is,
> That go on pilgrimage;
> Here little, and hereafter bliss,
> Is best from age to age.

Towards the end, in the 'enchanted ground', they meet Mr Valiant-for-Truth, sword in hand, with the scars of battle still on him. Mr Greatheart commends him: 'Then this was your victory, even your faith,' Valiant-for-Truth replies: 'It was so. I believed, and therefore came out, got into the way, fought all that set themselves against me, and, by believing, am come to this place.' 'Who would true valour see, let him come hither', celebrating such constancy, follows immediately. We give here the original version.[2]

When he is summoned to cross the River, Mr Valiant-for-Truth leaves us with a haunting challenge: 'though with great difficulty I have got hither, yet now I do not repent me of all the troubles I have been at to arrive where I am. My sword I give to him that shall succeed me in my pilgrimage, and my courage and skill to him that can get it. My marks and scars I carry with me . . .'

---

[1] *The Pilgrim's Progress*, ed. H. Ross Williamson (HarperCollins, London, 1979) pp. 246–7.

[2] Ibid., pp. 303–4.

Who would true valour see,
Let him come hither;
One here will valiant be,
Come wind, come weather;
There's no discouragement
Shall make him once relent
His first avow'd intent
To be a pilgrim.

Whoso beset him round
With dismal stories,
Do but themselves confound;
His strength the more is.
No lion can him fright,
He'll with a giant fight,
But he will have a right
To be a pilgrim.

Hobgoblin nor foul fiend
Can daunt his spirit;
He knows he at the end
Shall life inherit.
Then fancies fly away,
He'll not fear what men say;
He'll labour night and day
To be a pilgrim.

(Original text from *The Pilgrim's Progress*)

Thomas Ken (1637–1711)

In the midst of the shifting politics of the late seventeenth century in England, Bishop Ken stands as a staunch Laudian; that is, he believed the Anglican Church, as established by law, to be part of the universal Church Catholic, while yet acknowledging a loyalty to the Crown which was unswerving but outspoken in criticism. Thus, when chaplain to Charles II, he refused to allow Nell Gwynne to use his house, an act of boldness so admired by the King that, in 1684, he rewarded him with the bishopric of Bath and Wells. In 1687 he was one of the seven bishops who refused to read James II's Declaration of Indulgence, yet, believing in the Stuart divine right to the throne, he joined the 'non-juror' bishops in refusing to take the oath of loyalty to William of Orange. He was deprived of his See in 1691 and went into retirement. For a period he lived at Longleat where the Thynnes were the centre of a literary circle. Here this Catholic divine made friends with a staunch Independent, Walter Singer, and his poet daughter, Elizabeth, in Frome. Father and daughter were unusually ecumenical in their outlook, and Elizabeth both widened her literary horizons and gained a knowledge of Catholic theology from Bishop Ken.[1] For the rest of his days, Ken followed a studious ascetic way of life.

Early in his career Thomas Ken had taught at Winchester College and probably he wrote his famous morning and evening hymns for school worship there. The last verse in each is a form of the ancient doxology which, in Ken's translation, is now familiar in English worship. There is a tranquillity and cheerfulness in his simple verses which convey great assurance. This assurance of faith, it would seem, was his anchorage through all the storms of his life. It is little wonder that these two hymns became such favourites. They were included in the supplement to the Tate and Brady psalter of 1709 in a semi-official status. Ian Bradley has collected a number of anecdotes from nineteenth-century sources showing how ubiquitous was the use of the evening hymn in particular. These include a picture from Kipling of four young English engineers, building a railway across India, who kept up their spirits in a sweltering dust-storm by singing 'Glory to thee, my God, this night'.[2]

---

[1] See H.F. Stecher, *Elizabeth Rowe, the Poetess of Frome* (H.L. Burn, Peter Land, Frankfurt/M, 1972), pp. 68–72.

[2] Bradley, *Abide with Me*, p. 216.

Awake, my soul, and with the sun
Thy daily stage of duty run;
Shake off dull sloth, and joyful rise
To pay thy morning sacrifice.

Redeem thy mis-spent time that's past,
Live this day as if 'twere thy last:
Improve thy talent with due care;
For the great day thyself prepare.

Let all thy converse be sincere,
Thy conscience as the noon-day clear;
Think how all-seeing God thy ways
And all thy secret thoughts surveys.

Awake, awake, ye heavenly choir,
May your devotion me inspire,
That I like you my age may spend,
Like you may on my God attend.

Praise God, from whom all blessings flow,
Praise him, all creatures here below,
Praise him above, ye heavenly host,
Praise Father, Son, and Holy Ghost.   Amen.

ॐ

Glory to thee, my God, this night
For all the blessings of the light;
Keep me, O keep me, King of kings,
Beneath thy own almighty wings.

Forgive me, Lord, for thy dear Son,
The ill that I this day have done,
That with the world, myself and thee,
I, ere I sleep, at peace may be.

Teach me to live, that I may dread
The grave as little as my bed;
Teach me to die, that so I may
Rise glorious at the awful day.

O may my soul on thee repose,
And with sweet sleep my eyelids close,
Sleep that may me more vigorous make
To serve my God when I awake.

Praise God from whom all blessings flow,
Praise him all creatures here below,
Praise him above, ye heavenly host,
Praise Father, Son, and Holy Ghost.

Joseph Addison (1672–1719)

B y the early part of the eighteenth century the English intellectual establishment was becoming more cosmopolitan and urban; coming, in Addison's words, 'out of the closets and libraries, schools and colleges, to dwell in clubs and assemblies, tea-tables and coffee houses'. One of these was the Kit-Kat Club, set up by Whig supporters at the house of a well-known maker of cakes and pastries near the Temple Bar. Here men of all disciplines, the sciences, politics, literature and philosophy, could take cakes and coffee, gossip and exchange ideas. The circle included Addison himself, the authors Alexander Pope and Jonathan Swift, dramatists Joseph Congreve and John Vanbrugh and Richard Steele, soldier, writer, and social reformer, and founder of *The Tatler* and *The Spectator*, to which Addison contributed. Addison was an MP (1708–19) and held ministerial office in two Whig governments. He also wrote poetry and plays, and liked in his journalism to make ideas accessible to a wider public.

It was Addison the journalist who gave us three fine hymns. In *The Spectator* for 26 July 1712, he wrote an essay on 'Divine Providence' which ended with a versification of Psalm 23. On 9 August his essay on 'Gratitude' closed with verses beginning 'When all thy mercies, O my God'. On 23 August an essay on 'Faith and Devotion' culminated in his grand verses inspired by the beginning of Psalm 19.

'The Lord my pasture shall prepare' has the charm and balance of a pastoral landscape, perhaps as created by Capability Brown at Castle Howard or Blenheim Palace; there is no sense of a working shepherd. We are not likely to stumble over a serpent or encounter real death in such idyllic scenes. The style is literary: 'sultry glebes' lead to 'verdant landscapes' via 'dewy meads'. This 23rd Psalm is a long way from the simplicity of 'The Lord's my shepherd, I'll not want' of the Scottish Psalter's words some fifty years earlier; it is an art song more at home in the drawing room than among the chanting crowds at St Paul's Cross. Nevertheless we feel genuine care from the hands of a gracious and loving Lord.

The easygoing tune by Henry Carey matches his lines perfectly, with a gently flowing 3/4 time signature and phrases that balance each other – he adds some passing notes to smooth out the repeat of the first line and changes the rhythmic pattern from three even notes in a bar to a minim and two quavers, which gives just a little impetus for the song to return to the fold in the final lines.

SURREY

The Lord my pasture shall prepare,
And feed me with a shepherd's care;
His presence shall my wants supply,
And guard me with a watchful eye;
My noonday walks he shall attend,
And all my midnight hours defend.

When in the sultry glebe I faint,
Or on the thirsty mountain pant,
To fertile vales and dewy meads
My weary wandering steps he leads,
Where peaceful rivers, soft and slow,
Amid the verdant landscape flow.

Though in a bare and rugged way
Through devious lonely wilds I stray,
Thy bounty shall my pains beguile;
The barren wilderness shall smile
With sudden green and herbage crowned,
And streams shall murmur all around.

Though in the paths of death I tread,
With gloomy horrors overspread,
My steadfast heart shall fear no ill,
For thou, O Lord, art with me still:
Thy friendly staff shall give me aid,
And guide me through the dreadful shade.

Carey was about fifteen years younger than Addison. Most of his music was for the theatre and he wrote words as well as music for at least one ballad opera, *A Wonder, or the Honest Yorkshireman*.

The majestic lines of the next poem, 'The spacious firmament on high' sweeps us from the life of an eighteenth-century landed gentleman to the cosmos itself, a giant theatre of the universe. Here Addison stands between the medieval world-view and the new scientific order unveiled by Copernicus, Galileo and, closer to home, Isaac Newton. 'The spacious firmament on high' conjures up the old flat-roofed earth with heaven above it. But the universe is now alive with heavenly bodies that 'roll' in their given orbits, even if they still 'move round the dark, terrestrial ball'. Addison is not a scientist; his poetry has a passionate, almost mystical, element in its imagery. These heavens are not above: we are within them – part of the great audience that responds to a daily retelling of Creation's story. For they do, indeed, speak in their silence. With a typical eighteenth-century appeal to 'reason's ear' Addison proclaims his unshakeable theistic message. The tune was especially written for these words by Addison's contemporary, John Sheeles.

ADDISON'S LONDON

The spacious firmament on high,
With all the blue ethereal sky,
And spangled heavens, a shining frame,
Their great Original proclaim.
The unwearied sun from day to day
Does his Creator's power display,
And publishes to every land
The works of an almighty hand.

Soon as the evening shades prevail
The moon takes up the wondrous tale,
And nightly to the listening earth
Repeats the story of her birth;
Whilst all the stars that round her burn,
And all the planets in their turn,
Confirm the tidings, as they roll,
And spread the truth from pole to pole.

What though in solemn silence all
Move round the dark terrestrial ball;
What though nor real voice nor sound
Amid their radiant orbs be found;
In reason's ear they all rejoice,
And utter forth a glorious voice;
For ever singing as they shine,
'The hand that made us is divine.'

Addison's paean of gratitude for the goodness and mercy that have followed him, 'When all thy mercies O my God', has been called 'unequalled as a piece of spiritual biography'. Its gentle rhythm is well caught in Frederick Gore Ouseley's mid-Victorian tune.

When all thy mercies, O my God,
  My rising soul surveys,
Transported with the view, I'm lost
  In wonder, love, and praise.

Unnumbered comforts to my soul
  Thy tender care bestowed,
Before my infant heart conceived
  From whom those comforts flowed.

When in the slippery paths of youth
  With heedless steps I ran,
Thine arm unseen conveyed me safe,
  And led me up to man.

When worn with sickness oft hast thou
  With health renewed my face;
And when in sins and sorrows sunk,
  Revived my soul with grace.

Through every period of my life
  Thy goodness I'll pursue,
And after death in distant worlds
  The glorious theme renew.

Through all eternity to thee
  A joyful song I'll raise;
For O, eternity's too short
  To utter all thy praise.

PHILOSOPHIÆ

NATURALIS

PRINCIPIA

MATHEMATICA.

Autore *J S. NEWTON*, *Trin. Coll. Cantab. Soc.* Mathefeos
Profeſſore *Lucaſiano*, & Societatis Regalis Sodali.

IMPRIMATUR.
S. PEPYS, *Reg. Soc.* PRÆSES.
Julii 5. 1686.

LONDINI,

Juſſu *Societatis Regiæ* ac Typis *Joſephi Streater*. Proſtant Vena-
les apud *Sam. Smith* ad inſignia Principis *Walliæ* in Cœmiterio
D. *Pauli*, alioſq; nonnullos Bibliopolas. *Anno* MDCLXXXVII.

Title page of Newton's *Philosophia Naturalis Principia Mathematica*

Isaac Watts (1674–1748)

I saac Watts was offered the chance of a university education by a local benefactor but chose to go to one of the leading Dissenting academies at Stoke Newington (1709–14). This was directed by Thomas Rowe who, with his brother Benoni, an independent minister, represented the intellectual aspect of nonconformity. Watts eventually became pastor of the Independent church at Mark Lane in London but retired in 1712 because of poor health. His main vocation was as a writer of hymns, poems and educational works.

An illuminating detail of personal history concerns his friendship with Elizabeth Singer Rowe, a gifted young poet and devout Independent from Frome, Somerset. She married Thomas Rowe, son of the Stoke Newington principal, and lived in London from 1710 until 1715 when her husband died. She returned then to Frome where she made a name for herself as a prolific writer of poems and letters. Watts was obviously charmed by Elizabeth, to the point of writing romantic verses to her. More seriously, he became her spiritual and literary mentor. She acknowledged his influence in guiding her to less romantic, more uplifting themes in verses addressed 'to Mr Watts on his poems sacred to devotion':

> No gay Alexis in the grove,
> Shall be my future theme;
>
> . . .
>
> Seraphic heights I seem to gain
> And sacred transports feel
> While Watts to thy celestial strain
> Supriz'd I listen still.[1]

At a time when many dissenting congregations still thought it was frivolous to sing anything but psalms in church services, Watts set himself to liberate worship from the limitations of the Old Covenant by composing hymns which celebrated the New Covenant. At the same time he wrote for the ordinary worshipper, eschewing rhetorical devices. 'I would neither indulge in any bold metaphors,' he wrote, 'nor admit of hard words, nor tempt the ignorant worshipper to sing above his understanding.[2] His main collections were *Hymns and Spiritual Songs*

---

[1] See M. Reeves, *Pursuing the Muses: Female Education and Nonconformist Culture 1700–1900* (Leicester University Press, 1997), pp. 21, 24.
[2] Wakefield, *Dict. of Christian Spirituality, sub nom.*

(1707), *The Psalms of David* (1719) and the first children's hymn-book, *Divine Songs* (1715). Altogether he wrote about 750 hymns. The three hymns selected here reach the heights of his hymnody. 'O God, our help in ages past', based on Psalm 90, is written in short, plain words, yet it has a grand, monumental character which has made it *par excellence* the hymn for solemn national occasions, justifying the comment 'something of an event in British history'.

ST ANNE

O God, our help in ages past,
   Our hope for years to come,
Our shelter from the stormy blast,
   And our eternal home.

Under the shadow of thy throne
   Thy saints have dwelt secure;
Sufficient is thine arm alone,
   And our defence is sure.

Before the hills in order stood,
   Or earth received her frame,
From everlasting thou art God,
   To endless years the same.

A thousand ages in thy sight
   Are like an evening gone,
Short as the watch that ends the night
   Before the rising sun.

Time, like an ever-rolling stream,
   Bears all its sons away;
They fly forgotten, as a dream
   Does at the opening day.

O God, our help in ages past,
   Our hope for years to come,
Be thou our guard while troubles last,
   And our eternal home.

'When I survey the wondrous Cross' is equally plain in language: it needs no flowery similes to convey the immense poignancy of this Good Friday hymn – a poignancy which is heightened if we use the second line as Watts wrote it: 'Where the young Prince of glory died'.[1]

ROCKINGHAM

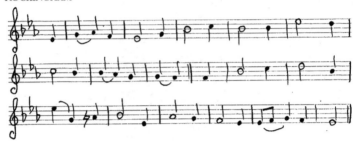

When I survey the wondrous Cross,
   On which the Price of glory died,
My richest gain I count but loss,
   And pour contempt on all my pride.

Forbid it, Lord, that I should boast
   Save in the death of Christ my God;
All the vain things that charm me most,
   I sacrifice them to his blood.

See from his head, his hands, his feet,
   Sorrow and love flow mingled down;
Did e'er such love and sorrow meet,
   Or thorns compose so rich a crown?

His dying crimson like a robe,
   Spreads o'er his body on the Tree;
Then am I dead to all the globe,
   And all the globe is dead to me.

Were the whole realm of nature mine,
   That were a present far too small;
Love so amazing, so divine,
   Demands my soul, my life, my all.

---

[1] Vera Brittain reports that this was Gandhi's favourite hymn. It was sung at his memorial service in London in 1947, thus linking 'the aged Apostle of non-violence with the young Prince of Peace'. *The Testament of Experience* (Fontana Paperbacks, London, 1980), p. 461.

Christ on the cold stone

'Give me the wings of faith to rise' is the evangelical vision of the communion of saints (compare with the medieval pictures of Bernard of Cluny★ and Peter Abelard★). There is a strong sense of spiritual aspiration which urges the singer onwards through the verses and this is enhanced by the new tune, *San Rocco* (Derek Williams, b. 1945) with its upward lilt on the last line of the melody to end on the fifth.

Give me the wings of faith to rise
  Within the veil, and see
The saints above, how great their joys,
  How bright their glories be.

Once they were mourning here below,
  And wet their couch with tears;
They wrestled hard, as we do now,
  With sins and doubts and fears.

I ask them whence their victory came;
  They, with united breath,
Ascribe their conquest to the Lamb,
  Their triumph to his death.

They marked the footsteps that he trod,
  His zeal inspired their breast,
And, following their incarnate God,
  Possess the promised rest.

Our glorious Leader claims our praise
  For his own pattern given;
While the long cloud of witnesses
  Show the same path to heaven.

Evangelical service at Surrey Chapel, early nineteeth century

Latin 17th Century, tr. F. Pott (1832–1909)

O ne of our most commonly sung Easter hymns is anonymous. The seventeenth-century Latin original was translated by Francis Pott, a Tractarian who became rector of Northill, Bedfordshire. The grave, bare language of this theologically-based hymn carries a majesty of its own which is enhanced by the tune adapted from the *Gloria* of Palestrina's *Magnificat Tertii Toni*. Monk added the 'Alleluya'. The hymn contrasts strikingly with Fortunatus's festive semi-pagan song on the one hand and Charles Wesley's★ personal outpouring on the other.

> The strife is o'er, the battle done;
> Now is the Victor's triumph won;
> O let the song of praise be sung.
> *Alleluya!*
>
> Death's mightiest powers have done their worst,
> And Jesus hath his foes dispersed;
> Let shouts of praise and joy outburst.
>
> On the third morn he rose again
> Glorious in majesty to reign;
> O let us swell the joyful strain.
>
> He brake the age-bound chains of hell;
> The bars from heaven's high portals fell;
> Let hymns of praise his triumph tell.
>
> Lord, by the stripes which wounded thee
> From death's dread sting thy servants free,
> That we may live, and sing to thee.

From Lyra Davidica *18th Century*

This favourite hymn, sung only on Easter Sunday, is also anonymous. It was translated from a Latin hymn *Surrexit Christus Hodie* from fourteenth-century Bohemia, the birthplace, a century later, of the reformer Jan Hus. Our modern words come from Arnold's *Compleat Psalmist* of 1749, but Bradley points out that verses two and three are very different from those in the original *Lyra Davidica* of 1708: 'Haste ye females from your fright, take to Galilee your flight; to his sad disciples say: Jesus Christ is risen today.[1]

Both this and the preceding hymn give congregations a chance to sing out the Hebrew exclamation *Hallelujah* ('Praise Jehovah') in its Latin form *Alleluia*. This refrain is a survivor of the elaborate *Alleluias* which were grafted on to earlier traditional plainsong, with suitably joyous music, for the Proper of the Roman Mass, the part which varies according to day and season.

> Jesus Christ is risen to-day, Alleluya!
> Our triumphant holy day, Alleluya!
> Who did once, upon the Cross, Alleluya!
> Suffer to redeem our loss. Alleluya!
>
> Hymns of praise then let us sing, Alleluya!
> Unto Christ, our heavenly King, Alleluya!
> Who endured the Cross and grave, Alleluya!
> Sinners to redeem and save. Alleluya!
>
> But the pains that he endured Alleluya!
> Our salvation have procured; Alleluya!
> Now above the sky he's King, Alleluya!
> Where the angels ever sing. Alleluya!

---

[1] Ian Bradley, *The Penguin Book of Hymns* (Penguin Books, London, 1990), p. 214.

Charles Wesley (1707–88) and John Wesley (1703–91)

Writing hymns and setting them to music was almost a cottage industry for the Wesley family, an astonishing dynasty whose gifts spanned three generations. A look through the index of a typical hymn-book gives us: John, collector, translator and publisher; Charles, who wrote the words of nearly 6000 hymns; Charles's son, also Charles, a musician and writer of hymn tunes; and finally his grandson, Samuel Sebastian, who has the greatest number of tunes; to his name. There should, perhaps, also be added Charles's eldest son Samuel (Old Sam), the finest composer of them all and best known for his organ voluntaries, antiphons and anthems such as the great *In exitu Israel*.

The husband of Charles and John's mother, Susannah, was a Church of England parson of the High Church tradition with a living in a small Lincolnshire village. Susannah's father had been a dissenting minister who used to discuss theology with her as a child; she brought up her own children in the same way. When John was ordained at Oxford it was a natural progression for him to gather together a group of friends whose aim was to improve the mind and strengthen character by study and self-discipline. On weekdays they read the New Testament and the classics; on Sundays they discussed religious topics. No moment was to be spent 'triflingly employed or in whiling away time.'[1] Many Oxford societies, then as now, regarded the whiling away of time as a necessary part of university life, hence this society became known as 'The Holy Club' or the 'Methodists' because of the way they 'methodized' every hour of the day. By 1730, the Club had begun preaching and ministering to the underprivileged; in particular to debtors imprisoned in the notorious Oxford Gaol. It seemed that John Wesley, now a fellow of Lincoln College with lectures to give and souls to save, had found his vocation in life.

But five years later, fate decided otherwise. Wesley was invited to go as chaplain to a group of settlers in the newly established colony of Georgia in North America. He and Charles, now also ordained, travelled out to America with a group of Moravian Protestant exiles. One can picture the two highly-

---

[1] Dorothy Marshall, *John Wesley* (Clarendon Biographies, OUP, 1965), p. 11.

educated young men sitting below deck in a sailing ship that battled with the elements, and finding common spiritual ground with a group of German-speaking carpenters, builders or farmers who were prepared to travel across the ocean in order to worship according to their conscience. Wesley was much impressed by the Moravians' calmness and faith in the midst of violent transatlantic gales. Together they prayed, studied the Bible and sang hymns from the German. This encounter proved to be a catalyst in the lives of the brothers, leading both to their own spiritual conversions and to the development of Methodism.

Come, O thou Traveller unknown,
Whom still I hold, but cannot see;
My company before is gone,
And I am left alone with thee;
With thee all night I mean to stay
And wrestle till the break of day.

I need not tell thee who I am,
My misery and sin declare;
Thyself hast called me by my name,
Look on thy hands and read it there:
But who, I ask thee, who art thou?
Tell me thy name, and tell me now.

In vain thou strugglest to get free;
I never will unloose my hold:
Art thou the Man that died for me?
The secret of thy love unfold:
Wrestling, I will not let thee go
Till I thy name, thy nature know.

Yield to me now, for I am weak,
But confident, in self-despair;
Speak to my heart, in blessings speak,
Be conquered by my instant prayer:
Speak, or thou never hence shalt move,
And tell me if thy name is Love.

'Tis Love, 'tis Love! Thou diedst for me!
I hear thy whisper in my heart;
The morning breaks, the shadows flee,
Pure, universal Love thou art:
To me, to all, thy mercies move;
Thy nature and thy name is Love.

Charles Wesley's turning point came soon after returning from Georgia, when he was ill in bed; John's a few months later as he was listening to a reading of Martin Luther's preface to the *Epistle to the Romans*. All his life he had struggled to find salvation through 'good works'. Now he found it through faith. In a now famous expression, he wrote: 'I felt my heart strangely warmed, I felt that I did trust in Christ, Christ alone, for salvation; and assurance was given me, that he had taken away *my* sins, even *mine*, and saved *me* from the law of sin and death.' From that moment in May 1738, the mission in Britain began. Although, at his death, John Wesley still called himself a High Churchman of the Church of England, his enduring legacy was the setting up of a church with different priorities, a society based on compassion which preached the gospel to outsiders, the ignorant and the underclass. Today their Methodist Church has spread to every continent and has influenced all branches of the Christian church.

Of the two brothers, John was the scholar, preacher, organizer and man of action, preaching over 40,000 sermons, travelling 250,000 miles, writing 233 original works and editing 100 more, including various collections of hymns. Charles was the poet, also an active preacher, and the more imaginative and flexible of the two, foreseeing that Methodism had to separate from the Anglican church if it was to have enough priests to administer the sacraments and enough lay-ministers to preach to the thousands of people who flocked to fields and purpose-built chapels in order to hear the message of forgiveness and salvation.

From earliest days Methodist congregations were encouraged to join in singing hymns in contrast to High Anglican worship, where choral music was still performed by the choir. John Wesley had been much impressed by the Moravian singing, and became convinced that good hymns, powerfully sung, would give an added dimension to the spiritual and emotional needs of his congregation; they were also a way of teaching church doctrine. In his methodical way, he set about collecting and translating hymns and tunes from all sources, while Charles began his astonishing output of verse. John's first hymn collection appeared in 1737, in South Carolina. It included metrical psalms, six poems by George Herbert* and 33 hymns by Isaac Watts.* Forty-three years later he published his final work, the *Collection of Hymns for the Use of the People called Methodists*, which he said was 'large enough to contain all the important truths of our most holy religion'.[1]

John Wesley preaching

The three hymns we have chosen can only give a suggestion of the breadth of Charles Wesley's vision. 'Come, O thou Traveller unknown' comes from a longer poem based on the story of Jacob's wrestling with the angel in Genesis 32:24–30. It is very personal, reflecting perhaps the struggle that both brothers had to find their faith. 'O thou who camest from above' is, in contrast, an invocation of the divine fire, the Holy Spirit, to burn on the 'mean altar' of the heart, so that all its acts might be inspired from the holy fire within. The tune is attributed to Charles's grandson, Samuel Sebastian Wesley, but its eighteenth-century style is similar to the *Ave Regina* of his father, 'Old Sam', and Samuel Sebastian may only have added to Old Sam's original.

Charles Wesley's third hymn is an outward looking song for Easter. John Wesley chose for it a joyful tune from a chorale book of the Moravian Hussites, from Herrnhut in Saxony.

---

[1] Dorothy Marshall, *op. cit.* p. 25.

O thou who camest from above,
 The pure celestial fire to impart,
Kindle a flame of sacred love
 On the mean altar of my heart.

There let it for thy glory burn
 With inextinguishable blaze,
And trembling to its source return
 In humble prayer, and fervent praise.

Jesus, confirm my heart's desire
 To work, and speak, and think for thee;
Still let me guard the holy fire,
 And still stir up thy gift in me.

Ready for all thy perfect will,
 My acts of faith and love repeat,
Till death thy endless mercies seal,
 And make my sacrifice complete.

SAVANNAH

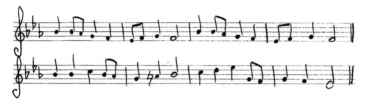

Love's redeeming work is done;
Fought the fight, the battle won:
Lo, our Sun's eclipse is o'er!
Lo, he sets in blood no more!

Vain the stone, the watch, the seal,
Christ has burst the gates of hell;
Death in vain forbids his rise;
Christ has opened Paradise.

Lives again our glorious King;
Where, O Death, is now thy sting?
Dying once, he all doth save;
Where thy victory, O grave?

Soar we now where Christ has led,
Following our exalted Head;
Made like him, like him we rise;
Ours the cross, the grave, the skies.

Hail the Lord of earth and heaven!
Praise to thee by both be given:
Thee we greet triumphant now;
Hail, the Resurrection thou!

Cologne 1710, tr. T.A. Lacey (1853–1931)

I n their return to ancient hymn texts, the Victorian 'antiquarian' school searched as close to the first centuries of Christian worship as possible. Although the actual text of this Advent hymn only dates from the eighteenth century, it was based on ancient Advent Antiphons dating from the ninth century or earlier. This brought them close to the Jewish inheritance of the Christian church. Thus 'O come, O come, Emmanuel', like 'The God of Abraham praise'★, represents our debt to Jewish spirituality, even though the two hymns were created under different circumstances. Each verse evokes one of the many great images under which the unnameable God could be approached. The last two lines, using the metaphor of the Corner-stone, brings together the Old and New Dispensations. Reference to the stone which the builders rejected, and which has become the head of the corner, is found in Luke 20:17, going back to Psalm 118:22 and Isaiah 28:16, while this is picked up as a figure of Christ in Ephesians 2:20 and 1 Peter 2:6. It also inspired a Latin Office Hymn of the seventh century, translated as 'Christ is our corner-stone' (NEH 206).

The tune is a melody adapted from a French missal by Thomas Helmore★ (1811–90). He was the Master of the Choristers of the Chapel Royal and worked with J. M. Neale★ in finding appropriate tunes for Neale's Greek and Latin translations. He campaigned vigorously to persuade congregations to revert to Gregorian plainsong, and for this purpose published a *Manual of Plainsong* in 1849. His zeal for promoting 'right' hymns and tunes in parish worship finally led him to become vice-principal of the Anglican church's first teacher-training college, St Mark's and St John's, Chelsea. Here, singing was strongly emphasized and Helmore set out to train teachers in 'proper' church music so that they could form and train the new-style parish choirs.[1]

---

[1] Bradley, *Abide with Me*, p. 202.

Veni, veni, Emmanuel

O come, O come, Emmanuel!
Redeem thy captive Israel,
That into exile drear is gone
Far from the face of God's dear Son.
Rejoice! Rejoice Emmanuel
Shall come to thee, O Israel.

O come, thou Wisdom from on high!
Who madest all in earth and sky,
Creating man from dust and clay:
To us reveal salvation's way.

O come, O come, Adonaï,
Who in thy glorious majesty
From Sinai's mountain, clothed with awe,
Gavest thy folk the ancient law.

O come, thou Root of Jesse! draw
The quarry from the lion's claw;
From those dread caverns of the grave,
From nether hell, thy people save.

O come, thou Lord of David's Key!
The royal door fling wide and free;
Safeguard for us the heavenward road,
And bar the way to death's abode.

O come, O come, thou Dayspring bright!
Pour on our souls thy healing light;
Dispel the long night's lingering gloom,
And pierce the shadows of the tomb.

O come, Desire of nations! show
Thy kingly reign on earth below;
Thou Corner-stone, uniting all,
Restore the ruin of our fall.

Thomas Olivers (1725–99), from the Yigdal of Meir Leon

The changes taking place in the music of the Christian churches in the seventeenth and eighteenth centuries were to some extent parallelled by those in the Jewish synagogues. Both were abandoning the fluid chanting and modes of Gregorian plainsong and oriental Judaism in favour of rhythmic melodic forms, either in a traditional folk or a contemporary art style. In the Protestant churches the impetus for collections of music, especially hymns, came from religious reformers such as Luther, Calvin and Wesley, and their followers. In the synagogue, which had no equivalent reform movement, it was the *chazzan* or precentor who was responsible for musical development.

The *chazzanim* themselves, though fine singers, usually came from an oral tradition where music was not written down, so they relied on the synagogue's professional singers to provide them with new music. In eighteenth-century Berlin, however, the *chazzan* Ahron Beer (1738–1821), who not only had a fine tenor voice but was trained in music theory, collected together over 1200 religious tunes currently in use in synagogues throughout Europe. Twelve of these came from the repertoire of Meir Leon, the leading singer at the Duke's Place Synagogue in London where, in the words of the music historian A. Z. Idelsohn, 'His sweet voice and wonderful singing attracted a great attendance of even gentiles.'[1]

One of those Gentiles was Thomas Olivers, a Wesleyan minister and jobbing cobbler of Welsh parentage (though working in London) who had been converted by George Whitefield, one of the early founders of Methodism. He was so enraptured at hearing Leon sing an ancient Hebrew hymn from the *Yigdal* that he resolved to have it sung in church. The *Jewish Chronicle* of 1873 describes the event in the words of a contemporary Methodist:

---

[1] A. Z. Idelsohn, *Jewish Music in its Historical Development* (Schocken Books, New York 1967), p. 220.

Torah scroll (detail)

'During a conference in Wesley's time, Thomas Olivers, one of the preachers, came down to [my father] and, unfolding a manuscript, said, 'Look at this, I have rendered it from the Hebrew, giving it as far as I could a Christian character, and I have called on Leoni the Jew who has given me a synagogue melody to suit it; here is the tune, and it is to be called Leoni.' I read the composition and it was that now well-known grand imitation of Israel's ancient hymns – 'The God of Abraham, Praise'.[1]

The hymn was first published in 1772 and reached its 30th edition by 1799. In modern hymnals the words have been modified and the original ten verses cut down to eight, a move which has rather emasculated the power of Olivers's words, especially in the alteration of his first verse with its reference to Jehovah, great I am', which we have included here.

The text of the *Yigdal* is loosely based on Maimonides's *Thirteen Principles of Judaism*. A version of it still forms a Jewish hymn sung at the sabbath evening service. The original *Yigdal* melody was a variation of an old folk-motif which is common to Jewish, Spanish-Basque and Slav music.

LEONI

---

[1] Ibid., p. 221.

The God of Abraham praise,
  Who reigns enthroned above,
Ancient of everlasting days,
    And God of love:
  Jehovah, great I AM!
  By earth and heaven confessed;
We bow and bless the sacred name,
    Forever blessed.

The God of Abraham praise,
  At whose supreme command
From earth we rise and seek the joys
    At his right hand:
  We all on earth forsake,
  Its wisdom, fame and power,
And him our only portion make,
    Our shield and tower.

The God of Abraham praise,
  Whose all-sufficient grace
Shall guide us all our happy days,
    In all our ways.
  He is our faithful friend;
  He is our gracious God;
And he will save us to the end,
    Through Jesus' blood.

The whole triumphant host
  Give thanks to God on high:
'Hail, Father, Son and Holy Ghost'
    They ever cry.
  Hail, Abraham's God and mine!
  (We join the heavenly lays)
And celebrate with all our powers,
    His endless praise.

Latin 18th Century,
tr. Frederick Oakeley (1802–80)

No midnight service on Christmas Eve would be complete without the singing of 'O come, all ye faithful' (*Adeste, fideles*). The first chords from the organ kindle a special response of elation as we rise to join the thronging faithful from all down the ages. So it is strange that the origins of this special hymn are so obscure. Although written in Latin, it was not a medieval Office Hymn. It is reputed to be a French or German hymn of the eighteenth century.

The English translation is by Frederick Oakeley, published first in *Murray's Hymnal* in 1852. Oakeley, with Redhead and Helmore★, worked together as a trio to restore what they regarded as authentic church worship. They sought to revive the observance of feast days, to restore Gregorian and Anglican chant, and to promote the use of Tudor settings of the Eucharist. To counter what Helmore called 'frivolous' modern tunes, they unearthed tunes from older traditions. Oakely himself first developed his ideas of proper worship in the Margaret Chapel, Marylebone, where he was rector from 1839. This later became the famous centre of Anglo-Catholic worship at All Saints, Margaret Street. Criticism of his ritualistic practices finally led him to embrace Roman Catholicism in 1845. He became a canon of Westminster Cathedral.

ADESTE FIDELES

Adeste, fideles

O come, all ye faithful,
Joyful and triumphant,
O come ye, O come ye to Bethlehem;
Come and behold him
Born the King of Angels:
O come, let us adore him,
O come, let us adore him,
O come, let us adore him, Christ the Lord!

God of God,
Light of Light,
Lo! he abhors not the Virgin's womb;
Very God,
Begotten, not created:

See how the Shepherds,
Summoned to his cradle,
Leaving their flocks, draw nigh with lowly fear;
We too will thither
Bend our joyful footsteps:

Lo! star-led chieftains,
Magi, Christ adoring,
Offer him incense, gold, and myrrh;
We to the Christ Child
Bring our heart's oblations:

Child, for us sinners
Poor and in the manger,
Fain we embrace thee, with awe and love;
Who would not love thee,
Loving us so dearly?

Sing, choirs of Angels,
Sing in exultation,
Sing, all ye citizens of heaven above;
Glory to God
In the Highest:

Yea, Lord, we greet thee,
Born this happy morning,
Jesu, to thee be glory given;
Word of the Father,
Now in flesh appearing:

William Williams of Pantacelyn (1717–94)

I t is strange that, from a nation so given to song, English hymn collections mostly include only one Welsh hymn. But this is an outstanding representative of the fine tradition of biblically-based piety which developed in Wales in the post-Reformation period.[1] This was much influenced, *inter alia*, by the psalm renderings of Edmund Prys (1544–1623).

William Williams, though ordained in the Anglican church, was caught up in the Welsh evangelical revival and became an itinerant preacher in the Welsh Methodist connection. Our hymn is one of a large number which he wrote. It represents the first, third and fifth verses of the original, as translated in the first place by Peter Williams (1727–96). It has given us what may be the grandest re-enactment in modern hymnody of the Israelite journey through the barren wilderness to the Promised Land which is the type of all spiritual pilgrimage. Past generations of adults with their Bibles, and children in Sunday School, have fed on this great story (Exodus 13–17; Joshua 1–4). Modern hymn collections generally substitute 'Redeemer' for 'Jehovah' in the first line, both to link the Old Dispensation with the New and to meet Jewish scruples about using the sacred name. The hymn needs a Welsh tune: *Cym Rhondda* was composed by John Hughes (1873–1932) for a Welsh song festival. Sung in churches and chapels, at football matches or wherever, it swings along at a proper pace for a people marching towards Jordan. One of the authors remembers the choir tenor in a Baptist chapel trilling out the tenor part in the last line and hanging on lovingly to the last high note until firmly nudged along to the repeat by the organist!

A literal translation from the Welsh of the opening lines of our hymn runs:

> Lord, lead through the wilderness
> me a wretched-looking pilgrim
> with no strength or life in him
> as if lying in the grave.
> Almighty is the one who will lift me up.
>
> (Translated by Richard Jeffery)

---

[1] On Welsh spirituality, see Wakefield, *Dict. of Christian Spirituality*, under 'Welsh Spirituality'.

Guide me, O Thou great Jehovah,
  Pilgrim through this barren land;
I am weak, but Thou art mighty;
  Hold me with Thy powerful hand:
    Bread of heaven,
  Feed me now and evermore.

Open now the crystal fountain,
  Whence the healing stream doth flow;
Let the fiery, cloudy pillar
  Lead me all my journey through:
    Strong deliverer,
  Be Thou still my strength and shield.

When I tread the verge of Jordan,
  Bid my anxious fears subside:
Death of death, and hell's destruction,
  Land me safe on Canaan's side:
    Songs of praises
  I will ever give to Thee.

John Newton (1725–1807)

J ohn Newton was, perhaps, the most unclerical person to take holy orders in the eighteenth century. His story, told in his own autobiography, reads 'like a fantastic fairy tale'.[1] His dynamic energy led him from an extreme bout of adolescent religiosity to the riotous, blasphemous excesses of an eighteenth-century sailor. He never did anything by halves. After deserting his ship for a passionate love affair, he was press-ganged, brought back in chains, publicly flogged and reduced from midshipman to common sailor. Filled with rage, he became quite unmanageable and finally escaped off the west coast of Africa to work for a planter. But this was a case of from frying pan to fire. His master treated him worse than a slave and, at one stage, he was reduced almost to the status of an animal. Some memories of civilized life, however, lingered. Somehow he had kept a tattered geometry book in his pocket and he would creep out at night to draw arcs and triangles in the sand by moonlight. He began to go native in his life but, unexpectedly, a ship brought him a letter from his father and he determined to go home. His mood was bitter and disillusioned, his language profane, but his energy still sought a worthier outlet. A violent storm which nearly wrecked the ship on her voyage home suddenly showed him that all the objects he had pursued were worthless except the religion of his childhood.

For some years after, he led a respectable life, serving as a mate and then captain on a line of slave-trading ships. He was faithful in devotions and tried to improve his mind by learning Latin from a pocket Horace. But conventional eighteenth-century religion did not engage his whole personality. He needed 'a doctrine that would demand the absolute surrender of every energy of his mind and body'. In 1754 he suddenly found this in Evangelicalism and instantly gave himself with flaming energy to this faith. The rest of his life revolved around his new-found commitment, first at sea and later as a priest. He did not, apparently, regard slave-trading as wrong but only as distracting from his main purpose. Understandably, he had difficulty in persuading any bishop to ordain him but he achieved this finally and was presented to the living of Olney, where he worked for seventeen years. Here all the vitality which had enabled him to survive so many tribulations became

---

[1] David Cecil, *The Stricken Deer or the Life of Cowper* (Constable, London, 1929), p. 111. The material for this sketch is mainly drawn from Cecil's account of Newton's life, pp. 111–22.

focused on a whirlwind ministry of preaching, teaching, praying and writing. He galvanized into evangelical action everyone he met, including poor William Cowper★. It was Cowper's poetic inspiration which gave him the idea of publishing the Olney hymn-book for use in his weeknight prayer-meetings. When Cowper's genius gave out, Newton, the extrovert, wrote 280 hymns to complete the collection. Some of Newton's hymns come off triumphantly but many are simply hack pieces. He could be arrogant in his complete certainty, but his energy never flagged. His best-known hymn 'How sweet the name of Jesus sounds', typifies the personal faith which was the essence of evangelical spirituality.

> How sweet the name of Jesus sounds
>   In a believer's ear!
> It soothes his sorrows, heals his wounds,
>   And drives away his fear.
>
> It makes the wounded spirit whole,
>   And calms the troubled breast;
> 'Tis manna to the hungry soul,
>   And to the weary rest.
>
> Dear name! the rock on which I build,
>   My shield and hiding-place,
> My never-failing treasury filled
>   With boundless stores of grace.
>
> Jesus! my Shepherd, Brother, Friend,
>   My Prophet, Priest, and King,
> My Lord, my Life, my Way, my End,
>   Accept the praise I bring.
>
> Weak is the effort of my heart,
>   And cold my warmest thought;
> But when I see thee as thou art,
>   I'll praise thee as I ought.
>
> Till then I would thy love proclaim
>   With every fleeting breath;
> And may the music of thy name
>   Refresh my soul in death.

'Amazing Grace' has been matched by an equally effective Scottish–American folk melody. The words appeared in his Olney hymn-book and its theme of grace and hope seems to have spoken particularly to men and women in the United States, especially to African-American Christians still under the shadow of slavery. The rich harmonies of their great choirs bring out the hymn's great message to the full.

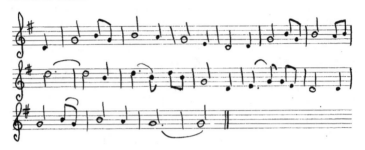

Amazing grace! how sweet the sound
  That saved a wretch like me!
I once was lost, but now am found,
  Was blind, but now I see.

'Twas grace that taught my heart to fear,
  And grace my fears relieved.
How precious did that grace appear
  The hour I first believed.

Through many dangers, toils and snares,
  I have already come;
'Tis grace hath brought me safe thus far,
  And grace will lead me home.

When we've been there ten thousand years
  Bright shining as the sun,
We've no less days to sing God's praise
  Than when we've first begun.

AUSTRIA

Glorious things of thee are spoken,
   Sion, city of our God;
He whose word cannot be broken
   Formed thee for his own abode:
On the Rock of Ages founded,
   What can shake thy sure repose?
With salvation's walls surrounded,
   Thou may'st smile at all thy foes.

See, the streams of living waters,
   Springing from eternal love,
Well supply thy sons and daughters,
   And all fear of want remove:
Who can faint, while such a river
   Ever flows their thirst to assuage?
Grace, which like the Lord the giver,
   Never fails from age to age.

Saviour, if of Sion's city
   I through grace a member am,
Let the world deride or pity, I will glory in thy name:
   Fading is the worldling's pleasure,
All his boasted pomp and show;
   Solid joys and lasting treasure
None but Sion's children know.

William Cowper (1731–1800)

I n his moving biography, Lord David Cecil describes Cowper's portrait
thus:

> The face is a plain, everyday sort of face with ... a wide, gentle mouth. The set
> of the lips, precise yet kindly, shows refinement, but it is an old maidish kind of
> refinement ... But out of this face glance a pair of eyes which change its whole
> expression; startled, speaking eyes ... the eyes of an artist, of a seer, can it be of a
> madman? This duality is the central fact of Cowper's life.[1]

A golden childhood was abruptly terminated at the age of six by the death of
his beloved mother, followed by an experience of bullying in his first school
which left him locked in an icy terror. His spirit was maimed for life and,
though for much of the time he could keep the horror at bay by the pleasant
socialities he loved, it always lurked in the background. For a time he found
comfort in the serene faith of George Herbert. Although educated as a lawyer,
he had no heart to practise his profession. Instead he sat idle in his rooms at the
Temple in mounting self-disgust. At the age of 31 he resolved on suicide but
could not bring himself to commit the act. In anguish he wrote lines of self-
condemnation:

> Damned below Judas; more abhorred than he was,
> Who for a few pence sold his holy Master!
> Twice betrayed, Jesus me the last delinquent,
> Deems the profanest.[2]

The powers of darkness had beaten him: he collapsed into madness and spent
the next year at Dr Cotton's Home for Madmen.

The decorous, formal religion of eighteenth-century England could not
save him. It was the emotional fervour of the Evangelical Movement that
loosened the iron grip of damnation and lifted the weight of horror from his
heart. The mystery of conversion happened silently: 'In a moment I believed
and received the Gospel'. Cowper found the security and tranquility, so long
ago snatched from him, in the household of the Unwins, a cultivated
evangelical family living in Huntingdon. Later, John Newton★, the dynamic

---

[1] The material for this sketch is largely drawn from David Cecil's study of Cowper (ref. under
Newton), see p. 15.

[2] Ibid., p. 69.

sailor-turned-clergyman, persuaded Cowper and the widowed Mrs Unwin, (who had become Cowper's substitute mother) to move to his parish at Olney in Buckinghamshire where, during his remaining years of sanity, he lived a life of piety and good works, writing poems and sometimes preaching.

The two hymns selected here set the man 'with eyes of a seer' beside the troubled, searching soul. 'God moves in a mysterious way' paints a tremendous picture of God striding the sea like a colossus (with a strange echo of Cleopatra's eulogy of Antony: 'his legs bestride the ocean: his reared arm crested the world). He is the unfathomable Designer, the Rider on the Storm. Cowper, the timid soul, urges fellow Christians to keep their courage up, yet, in the second hymn, he cannot apparently find 'a calm and heavenly frame' for himself. His poignant longing for a 'calm and heavenly frame' and fierce desire to tear out his 'dearest idol' speak eloquently to us. Alas, the gift of serene faith finally deserted him. By January 1773 he had succumbed again to a deep depression, convinced that he was irrevocably damned. Though he never really recovered his sanity, his friends brought him back to a relatively tranquil life in which nature and his pet hares (Bess, Puss and Tiny) played a healing part. In a sense the 'holy Dove ... sweet messenger of rest' *did* return.

God moves in a mysterious way
    His wonders to perform;
He plants his footsteps in the sea,
    And rides upon the storm.

Deep in unfathomable mines
    Of never-failing skill
He treasures up his bright designs,
    And works his sovereign will.

Ye fearful saints, fresh courage take,
    The clouds ye so much dread
Are big with mercy, and shall break
    In blessings on your head.

Judge not the Lord by feeble sense,
    But trust him for his grace;
Behind a frowning providence
    He hides a smiling face.

His purposes will ripen fast,
    Unfolding every hour;
The bud may have a bitter taste,
    But sweet will be the flower.

Blind unbelief is sure to err,
    And scan his work in vain;
God is his own interpreter,
    And he will make it plain.

CAITHNESS

O for a closer walk with God,
  A calm and heavenly frame;
A light to shine upon the road
  That leads me to the Lamb!

Return, O holy Dove, return,
  Sweet messenger of rest;
I hate the sins that made thee mourn,
  And drove thee from my breast.

The dearest idol I have known,
  Whate'er that idol be,
Help me to tear it from thy throne,
  And worship only thee.

So shall my walk be close with God,
  Calm and serene my frame;
So purer light shall mark the road
  That leads me to the Lamb.

William Blake (1757–1827)

W illiam Blake is one of those artists about whom it is almost impossible to write in a conventional way because the facts tell only part of the story. His mother and father kept a hosier's shop in Broad Street, central London, and he spent most of his life in that neighbourhood. Dissenters in religion and radical in politics, Blake's parents imbued young William with a sense of piety, knowledge of the Bible and the need for self-improvement and hard work. At the age of ten his parents sent him to drawing school; at 15 a master engraver took him as apprentice and, at 21, he won a place at the newly established Royal Academy Schools in Piccadilly. For the rest of his life, Blake survived on the fringes of poverty, practising his laborious trade as an 'engraver, a journeyman with wild notions' with 'a propensity for writing unintelligible verse'.[1]

Blake's inner life was as real for him as the desolation he found in London's streets and their grim workshops and chimneys. As a child he saw visions and, out of them, he wove fantasies which later took shape in epic poems such as *Milton* and *Jerusalem*. Once, when drawing tombs in Westminster Abbey, he saw its aisles and galleries filled with a procession of monks and priests singing plainsong and swinging thuribles of incense. Such experiences continued throughout his life. Blake had, it seems, eidetic perception, which means that he experienced abstract ideas or metaphors as actual people or angels who were with him in his own physical space.

In his twenties, Blake discovered the work of Emmanuel Swedenborg, a Swedish philosopher living in London who seemed to reinforce many of his own beliefs. The most important concerned the nature of humanity – the belief that Man, created in God's image, is, in his true nature, divine and that the material world reflects or contains a threefold sense of the divine – celestial, spiritual and natural – which is revealed through alchemy and occult rites but placed within the Christian context of redemption.

Blake believed that the human soul is made up of two opposing sides: the innocence of childhood and the experience of adulthood. One of

---

[1] The material for this account is mainly drawn from Peter Ackroyd, *Blake* (Sinclair-Stevenson, London, 1995).

the Songs of Innocence, the poem 'To Mercy, Pity, Peace and Love' is now sung as a hymn. In the original engravings figures representing these qualities are grouped around the words, a personification reinforced by Blake's use of capital letters for 'Mercy, Pity' etc. The poem is printed today as a hymn without the last verse, with its reference to 'heathen, Turk, or Jew'.

To Mercy, Pity, Peace, and Love,
    All pray in their distress,
And to these virtues of delight
    Return their thankfulness.

For Mercy, Pity, Peace, and Love,
    Is God our Father dear;
And Mercy, Pity, Peace, and Love,
    Is Man, his child and care.

For Mercy has a human heart,
    Pity, a human face;
And Love, the human form divine,
    And Peace, the human dress.

Then every man, of every clime,
    That prays in his distress,
Prays to the human form divine:
    Love, Mercy, Pity, Peace.

The best known of Blake's hymns was inspired by a childhood vision of Joseph of Arimathea and the legend that Joseph had brought Jesus as a boy to live in Glastonbury in Somerset. It is now known as *Jerusalem*, but the original poem was untitled and comes not from his epic poem *Jerusalem* but from the introduction to his *Milton*. In this work, Blake sees himself as taking on the prophetic mantle of John Milton. Blake mistrusted, indeed hated, all science and philosophy which put reason above the poetic or prophetic. He wrote of Isaac Newton, 'save us from Newton's blindness'. His famous illustration, now in London's Tate Gallery, has Newton seated on a rock by a dark sea measuring on the ground with a pair of compasses as if unaware of the vast oceans beyond. Most modern scholars regard his views as unfair to Newton, who was as fascinated by the occult as Blake and who described his own lack of knowledge in imagery very similar to Blake's. Blake was equally hostile to the empirical philosophy of John Locke, seeing both as Satan's progeny:

Satan my youngest born, art thou not Prince of the Starry Hosts
And of the Wheels of Heaven, to turn the Mills day & Night?
Art thou not Newtons [sic] Pantocrator weaving the Woof of Locke
To Mortals thy Mills seem everything.

In *Jerusalem* Blake has transmuted the giant Albion flour mill on Blackfriars Road – the first great factory in London, burned to a blackened ruin in 1791 – into a metaphor of all he hated; the 'dark satanic mills' which the poet must fight with the burning weapons of inspiration and genius so as to create a new order: 'To build Jerusalem is to build a city of holy art in which the Divine Humanity creates works of bliss.'

The song has become almost a second national, not to say nationalist, anthem in England. It owes much of its power to the setting by Hubert Parry who discovered the words in the First World War and wrote his magnificent tune for a celebration of the cause of women's suffrage in the Albert Hall in 1916. The song later became the special anthem of Women's Institutes, and the fourth stanza was used as a slogan by the Guild of St Matthew, a Christian Socialist society. Parry wrote a broad opening to the piece, creating two verses out of the original four, so that the imaginative sweep of Blake's words is carried right through the song. It is now sung at great formal and informal public occasions, most notably the last night of the annual BBC Promenade Concerts at the Royal Albert Hall in London.

And did those feet in ancient time
    Walk upon England's mountains green?
And was the holy Lamb of God
    On England's pleasant pastures seen?

And did the countenance divine
    Shine forth upon our clouded hills?
And was Jerusalem builded here
    Among those dark satanic mills?

Bring me my bow of burning gold!
    Bring me my arrows of desire!
Bring me my spear! O clouds, unfold!
    Bring me my chariot of fire!

I will not cease from mental fight,
    Nor shall my sword sleep in my hand,
Till we have built Jerusalem
    In England's green and pleasant land.

Joseph Mohr (1792–1848)

On Christmas Eve, 1818, there was panic among the church leaders at St Nicholas Church, Oberndorf, upper Austria: the organ – by then essential to German festive worship – had broken down! Step forward assistant priest, Joseph Mohr, carol in hand. According to one story he had been moved to write it by the peace and beauty of the starlit villages of the surrounding mountains as he walked home. Immediately set to music by organist Franz Gruber, it was sung on Christmas morning to the accompaniment of a guitar. After Christmas the organ-builder, who came to repair the organ, seized on the carol and began to popularize it all round the district. By 1840, when it was first published in Austria, it was already well known.

Emily Elliott first translated it into English around 1858 for St Mark's Church in Brighton, and other translations have appeared since. It has caught on here in Christmas carol services probably because of its romantic feeling and the easy swing of its folksy tune which is so perfectly welded to the words. Erik Routley describes it as the epitome of 'the German Christmas, cosy and child-centred, which was fast becoming part of the English scene just when it was being composed'.[1] It has surely become part of our Christmas dream.

---

[1] Erik Routley, *The English Carol* (Herbert Jenkins, London, 1958), p. 202.

Silent Night

Silent night, holy night,
all is calm, all is bright,
round yon virgin mother and child;
holy infant, so tender and mild,
sleep in heavenly peace,
sleep in heavenly peace.

Silent night, holy night.
Shepherds quake at the sight,
glories stream from heaven afar
heav'nly hosts sing alleluia:
Christ the Saviour is born,
Christ the Saviour is born.

Silent night, holy night.
Son of God, love's pure light,
radiant beams from thy holy face,
with the dawn of redeeming grace:
Jesus, Lord, at thy birth,
Jesus, Lord at thy birth.

PART III

Nineteenth and Twentieth Centuries

Henry Francis Lyte (1793–1847)

'**A** bide with me' is probably as popular today as when it first appeared in *Hymns Ancient and Modern* set to *Eventide* by William Henry Monk★, the hymnal's music-editor. Lyte was vicar of the parish of Brixham, in Devon – one of many nineteenth-century parsons whose work appeared in the book. A poetry prize-winner at university, he had a large number of hymns to his credit. The two best known, 'Praise, my soul, the King of heaven' (NEH 436), with music by John Goss (1800–80), and 'Abide with me', have both found a place in civic occasions and rites of passage – weddings, funerals and memorial services. They owe a good deal to their musical settings because words and music work so well together. Monk was a skilled musician who could adapt and abridge for the English tongue music from other traditions, such as his setting of a German chorale for 'As with gladness men of old' (NEH 47). And while some of his tunes have a fresh simplicity, for example *Ethelwald* for Charles Wesley's 'Soldiers of Christ, arise' (NEH 449), he also wrote the more profound music for 'And now, O Father, mindful of the love' (NEH 273), which is sung during the administration of Holy Communion.

Monk chose a measured tempo for 'Abide with me' and gave the tune a limited vocal range, well suited to large congregations and outdoor crowds. In fact, although 'Abide with me' is usually associated with funerals and grave events, the hymn took on a very different audience when it became the opener for the English Football Association Cup Final in 1927, apparently with the approval of George V.[1] Some critics find the poem too sentimental, but many people feel it gives voice to a prayer and an acknowledgement of approaching death that all of us have to face.

---

[1] Bradley, *Abide with Me*, p. 225.

EVENTIDE

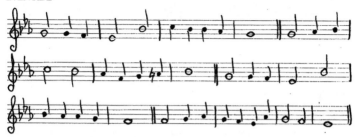

Abide with me; fast falls the eventide;
The darkness deepens; Lord, with me abide!
When other helpers fail, and comforts flee,
Help of the helpless, O abide with me.

Swift to its close ebbs out life's little day;
Earth's joys grow dim, its glories pass away;
Change and decay in all around I see;
O thou who changest not, abide with me.

I need thy presence every passing hour;
What but thy grace can foil the tempter's power?
Who like thyself my guide and stay can be?
Through cloud and sunshine, O abide with me.

I fear no foe with thee at hand to bless;
Ills have no weight, and tears no bitterness.
Where is death's sting? where, grave, thy
        victory?
I triumph still, if thou abide with me.

Hold thou thy cross before my closing eyes;
Shine through the gloom, and point me to the
        skies:
Heaven's morning breaks, and earth's vain
        shadows flee;
In life, in death, O Lord, abide with me!

John Henry Newman (1801–90)

Although Newman ended his life as a Cardinal in the Roman Catholic Church, his hymns have reached out beyond denominations. They are as familiar in a Protestant church in Northern Ireland as at High Mass in Westminster Cathedral. Although the style of his poems may appear simple, his understanding of the nature of religious faith has put him among the great Christian thinkers and apologists of the last two centuries.

Newman's life spans almost the whole of the nineteenth century. The Christian church he left was very different from the one in which he served his first ministry when, in 1828, as a fellow of Oriel college, he was given the living of the University Church of St Mary the Virgin, Oxford.[1] During this time he had an experience that transformed his life. In 1833, travelling in Italy, he suffered an extreme bout of scarlet fever which brought him near to death. On his way home, while becalmed on an orange-boat sailing from Palermo to Marseilles, he wrote a set of poems, later published in *Lyra Apostolica*. One of these, 'The Pillar of the Cloud', we now sing as 'Lead, kindly Light'. In the poem Newman expresses the doubts and uncertainties that were concerning him about his faith and his position in the Church of England.

In the same year John Keble, his colleague in Oxford, preached his famous Assize Sermon on National Apostasy, at St Mary's, calling for reform in the established Church of England. The immediate catalyst was the government's decision to suppress ten bishoprics in Ireland without consultation with the church. Keble denounced this control of Parliament and declared that the church was too 'liberal' in doctrine, having moved away both from early Christianity and the tenets of the Catholic Church. Newman soon became one of the leaders in what was to become the Oxford Movement, also known as Tractarianism, which published a series of *Tracts for the Times* covering a range of closely argued theological issues.

---

[1] Visitors to St Mary's Church notice the beautiful carved pulpit from which Newman preached his famous four o'clock sermons in the 1830s.

Nineteeth-century pulpit, University Church of St Mary the Virgin, Oxford

Lead, kindly Light, amid the encircling
    gloom,
  Lead thou me on;
The night is dark, and I am far from home,
  Lead thou me on.
Keep thou my feet; I do not ask to see
The distant scene; one step enough for me.

I was not ever thus, nor prayed that thou
    Shouldst lead me on;
I loved to choose and see my path; but now
    Lead thou me on.
I loved the garish day, and, spite of fears,
Pride ruled my will: remember not past years.

So long thy power hath blest me, sure it still
    Will lead me on
O'er moor and fen, o'er crag and torrent, till
    The night is gone,
And with the morn those angel faces smile,
Which I have loved long since, and lost awhile.

Newman's Tract 90 of 1841, which discussed the compatibility of the Thirty Nine Articles with Roman Catholic theology, aroused immense hostility among the liberals of the church, who also suspected that the Tractarians were leading their followers subversively towards Rome. There was a public outcry at its publication; the governing body of Oxford University condemned it and his bishop imposed on Newman a rule of silence. Newman spent some time in retreat at Littlemore, but a year later resigned his living and, in 1845, was received into the Roman Catholic faith.

After his ordination as a Roman Catholic priest, Newman moved away from his Oxford life, using his energies to promote his new faith in numerous writings, lectures and organizational duties, both as founder of the Oratory of Birmingham and, later, as rector of the new Catholic University in Dublin. Newman's best-known literary work is his *Dream of Gerontius*, published in 1866. In his vision, Gerontius, a symbolic figure of the wise man, sees the just soul leaving his body at the time of death. There are two moments in the poem where the visionary words of Newman still resound in our hymnals. The first is the soul's great affirmation of belief in the Christian faith: 'Firmly I believe and truly' – though the verse ending 'and her teaching as his own' is sometimes omitted by Protestant congregations. The second is the magnificent chorus of angels: 'Praise to the Holiest in the Height', so brilliantly set to music by Edward Elgar in his oratorio *The Dream of Gerontius*.

Firmly I believe and truly
  God is Three, and God is One;
And I next acknowledge duly
  Manhood taken by the Son.

And I trust and hope most fully
  In that Manhood crucified;
And each thought and deed unruly
  Do to death, as he has died.

Simply to his grace and wholly
  Light and life and strength belong,
And I love supremely, solely,
  Him the holy, him the strong.

And I hold in veneration,
  For the love of him alone,
Holy Church as his creation,
  And her teachings as his own.

Adoration ay be given,
  With and through the angelic host,
To the God of earth and heaven,
  Father, Son, and Holy Ghost.   Amen.

Praise to the Holiest in the height,
   And in the depth be praise,
In all his words most wonderful,
   Most sure in all his ways.

O loving wisdom of our God!
   When all was sin and shame,
A second Adam to the fight
   And to the rescue came.

O wisest love! that flesh and blood,
   Which did in Adam fail,
Should strive afresh against their foe,
   Should strive and should prevail;

And that a higher gift than grace
   Should flesh and blood refine,
God's presence and his very self,
   And essence all-divine.

O generous love! that he who smote
   In Man for man the foe,
The double agony in Man
   For man should undergo;

And in the garden secretly,
   And on the cross on high,
Should teach his brethren, and inspire
   To suffer and to die.

Praise to the Holiest in the height,
   And in the depth be praise,
In all his words most wonderful,
   Most sure in all his ways.

Alfred Tennyson (1809–92)

To many modern readers, with 'The Charge of the Light Brigade' ringing in their ears, Tennyson appears as the apotheosis of mid-to-late Victorian England. Poet Laureate from 1850 to his death, he has been seen to represent an establishment which glorified the 'Britishness' of the age as embodied in the gallantry of its soldiers, the rectitude of its moral standards and the firmness of its church-goers' faith. The truth, of course, about Tennyson and his age is not so simple. He was a boy when French imperialism under Napoleon was the dominant force in Europe. As a student he was strongly political, and his sympathies lay with European nationalist uprisings against despotic rule – a feeling shared by contemporaries such as Byron. By 1860, Tennyson was undoubtedly the most popular poet of his day with his public verse and epic poems anticipating the Pre-Raphaelites, but he had also written a number of personal and more introspective poems including the lyrics in *The Princess* and the long cycle *In Memoriam*.

The four stanzas of the hymn 'Strong Son of God' are from the prelude to *In Memoriam*. It was written between 1833 and 1850 in memory of Arthur Hallam, a close friend from Cambridge who died at the age of 22, two years after visiting the Pyrenees region with Tennyson in support of a Spanish nationalist movement. The poem cycle has its counterpart in Schubert's song-cycle *Winterreise*, with words by Wilhelm Müller; both poignantly express the grief, anger and despair of a young man who has lost his friend or loved one.

SONG 5

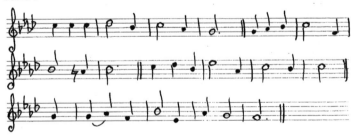

---

[1] *Oxford Comp. to Eng. Lit., sub tit.*

Strong Son of God, immortal Love,
    Whom we, that have not seen thy face,
    By faith, and faith alone, embrace,
Believing where we cannot prove:

Thou wilt not leave us in the dust;
    Thou madest man, he knows not why;
    He thinks he was not made to die:
And thou hast made him, thou art just.

Thou seemest human and divine,
    The highest, holiest manhood thou:
    Our wills are ours, we know not how;
Our wills are ours, to make them thine.

Our little systems have their day;
    They have their day and cease to be:
    They are but broken lights of thee,
And thou, O Lord, art more than they.

When *In Memoriam* was published in 1850, it was regarded as having a message of hope and affirmation of faith, but, as T. S. Eliot commented in 1936, 'It is not religious because of the quality of its faith, but because of the quality of its doubt ... [It] is a poem of despair of a religious kind.'[1] The opening verses chosen as a hymn echo the doubts of Newman's★ 'Lead, kindly Light', written at about the same time. The final stanzas give a more personal aspect to Tennyson's poem:

Forgive these wild and wandering cries,
    Confusions of a wasted youth;
    Forgive them where they fail in truth,
And in thy wisdom make me wise.

Forgive my grief for one removed,
    Thy creature, whom I found so fair.
    I trust he lives in thee, and there
I found him worthier to be loved.

F.W. Faber (1814–63)

F rederick Faber came up to Oxford from a Calvinist background but rapidly fell under the spell of Newman* and the High Church movement. He was ordained in the Anglican church and, as rector of Elton (1843), enthusiastically introduced many devotional practices from continental Catholicism. In 1845 he was received into the Roman Catholic church in which he was re-ordained as a priest in 1847. He took with him thirteen disciples and thought in terms of a new-style religious community. Eventually, under Cardinal Newman's guidance, he became the head of the new London Oratory, later the Brompton Oratory. He read widely, especially in the mystical tradition but, rather surprisingly, welcomed the advances of science. So his key theme became the wonders of God's power in creation and the wideness of his mercy to all creatures, juxtaposed with the infinite transcendence of the Godhead. He longed to bring new spiritual life to ordinary Victorian lay-people, and he wrote many hymns which were published in a collection in 1850. In the preface to this, he says his aim has been to do for English Catholics what the Olney* hymns had done for Protestants.

The two hymns selected here explore these themes with passion. 'There's a wideness in God's mercy' celebrates God's limitless creativity which embraces not only people of all creeds but a multitude of possible new worlds: 'There is grace enough for thousands of new worlds as great as this; there is room for fresh creations in that upper home of bliss.' That last phrase directs us towards the other theme of creaturely worship: the unfathomable God who is close to each one of us. Today the first theme calls us not to 'make his love too narrow by false limits of our own', while the second opens up a whole dimension of mysterious love beyond the reach of our technologies.

There's a wideness in God's mercy
  Like the wideness of the sea;
There's a kindness in his justice
  Which is more than liberty.

There is no place where earth's sorrows
  Are more felt than up in heaven;
There is no place where earth's failings
  Have such kindly judgement given.

For the love of God is broader
  Than the measure of man's mind;
And the heart of the Eternal
  Is most wonderfully kind

But we make his love too narrow
  By false limits of our own;
And we magnify his strictness
  With a zeal he will not own.

There is plentiful redemption
  In the blood that has been shed;
There is joy for all the members
  In the sorrows of the Head.

There is grace enough for thousands
  Of new worlds as great as this;
There is room for fresh creations
  In that upper home of bliss.

If our love were but more simple,
  We should take him at his word;
And our lives would be all gladness
  In the joy of Christ our Lord.

My God, how wonderful thou art,
  Thy majesty how bright,
How beautiful thy mercy-seat
  In depths of burning light!

How dread are thine eternal years,
  O everlasting Lord,
By prostrate spirits day and night
  Incessantly adored!

How wonderful, how beautiful,
  The sight of thee must be,
Thine endless wisdom, boundless power,
  And aweful purity!

O how I fear thee, living God,
  With deepest, tenderest fears,
And worship thee with trembling hope,
  And penitential tears!

Yet I may love thee too, O Lord,
  Almighty as thou art,
For thou hast stooped to ask of me
  The love of my poor heart.

No earthly father loves like thee,
  No mother, e'er so mild,
Bears and forbears as thou hast done
  With me thy sinful child.

Father of Jesus, love's reward.
  What rapture will it be
Prostrate before thy throne to lie,
  And gaze and gaze on thee.

St Mary Magdalen Church, Oxford

Mrs Cecil Frances Alexander, Née Humphries (1818–95)

'The redoubtable Mrs Alexander' she has been called. *Her Hymns for Little Children*, published in 1848, ran to more than 100 impressions in its first 50 years of use. Cecil Frances Humphries actually wrote most of her hymns before her marriage. She was born in Dublin, the daughter of an English army officer, and thus moved in the circle of the Anglo-Irish aristocracy. At 32 she married William Alexander, a cleric in the Church of Ireland who finally rose to the highest position as Archbishop of Armagh and Primate of Ireland.

Clearly she was by instinct a teacher, for her main focus as a hymn-writer was on the instruction of children in the fundamental theological truths of the Creed. Her 1848 collection was based on the catechism, containing fourteen hymns which specifically dealt with the various parts of the Apostles' Creed in simple language. 'All things bright and beautiful' interpreted the first affirmation: 'I believe in God the Father, Maker of heaven and earth.' 'Once in royal David's city' took up, of course, the Incarnation, and 'There is a green hill far away' expounded the Crucifixion. She wrote other hymns and, notably, showed affinity with Celtic spirituality in her translation of *St Patrick's Breastplate*★. Bradley has noted that in the first edition of *Hymns Ancient and Modern* there were eleven of her hymns and, in the *Church Hymnary*, fifteen.[1] Unlike some of the other women hymn-writers of this period, she did not write to express subjective personal experiences so much as objective doctrine and moral teaching. In 1849 she published *Moral Songs* for children.

Inevitably in a changing culture her views, both on society and on the upbringing of children, have run into criticism today. The famous verse in 'All things bright and beautiful' which pictures 'The rich man in his castle, the poor man at his gate, He made them high or lowly and ordered their estate', has now been dropped from hymn-books. It has come in for some fierce (sometimes amusing) criticism which has been documented by Bradley.[2] The hymn has some charming imagery from the natural world but perhaps gathering rushes by the water does not resonate with many children today. A

---

[1] Bradley, *Abide with Me*, p. 71.

[2] Ibid., p. 266.

third criticism concerns Mrs Alexander's inclination to teach good behaviour at every opportunity. Consider these lines in the original version of 'Once in royal David's city':

> Christian children all must be
> Mild, obedient, good as he.

In the *New English Hymnal* these lines have been eliminated and verses three and four revised to give a less feeble picture of the childhood of Jesus. As a model for today's youngsters, it still remains out of touch with our ideas of growing up today.

Once in royal David's city
　Stood a lowly cattle shed,
Where a mother laid her baby
　In a manger for his bed:
Mary was that Mother mild,
Jesus Christ her little Child.

He came down to earth from heaven
　Who is God and Lord of all,
And his shelter was a stable,
　And his cradle was a stall:
With the poor and mean and lowly,
Lived on earth our Saviour holy.

And through all his wondrous childhood
　Day by day like us he grew,
He was little, weak and helpless,
　Tears and smiles like us he knew:
And he feeleth for our sadness,
And he shareth in our gladness.

And our eyes at last shall see him
　Through his own redeeming love,
For that Child so dear and gentle,
　Is our Lord in Heaven above:
And he leads his children on
To the place where he is gone.

Not in that poor lowly stable,
　With the oxen standing by,
We shall see him: but in heaven,
　Set at God's right hand on high,
Where like stars his children crowned,
All in white shall wait around.

In spite of such strictures, many people remember 'All things bright and beautiful' as the cheerful hymn they sang in primary and Sunday school, while the opening line of 'Once in royal David's city' lingers long in the memory from the yearly carol service in King's College Chapel, Cambridge, on Christmas Eve.

> *All things bright and beautiful,*
> *All creatures great and small,*
> *All things wise and wonderful,*
> *The Lord God made them all.*

Each little flower that opens,
  Each little bird that sings,
He made their glowing colours,
  He made their tiny wings.

The purple-headed mountain,
  The river running by,
The sunset and the morning,
  That brightens up the sky;

The cold wind in the winter,
  The pleasant summer sun,
The ripe fruits in the garden,
  He made them every one;

The tall trees in the greenwood,
  The meadows for our play,
The rushes by the water,
  To gather every day;
He gave us eyes to see them,
  And lips that we might tell
How great is God Almighty,
  Who has made all things well.

There is a green hill far away,
　　Without a city wall,
Where the dear Lord was crucified
　　Who died to save us all.

We may not know, we cannot tell,
　　What pains he had to bear,
But we believe it was for us
　　He hung and suffered there.

He died that we might be forgiven,
　　He died to make us good;
That we might go at last to heaven,
　　Saved by his precious Blood.

There was no other good enough
　　To pay the price of sin;
He only could unlock the gate
　　Of heaven, and let us in.

O, dearly, dearly has he loved,
　　And we must love him too,
And trust in his redeeming Blood,
　　And try his works to do.

James Russell Lowell (1819–91)

Two contrasting currents of American culture influenced Victorian England and its hymnody: the evangelical fervour of Moody and Sankey* and the broad liberal aspirations of a rising intelligentsia. J. R. Lowell epitomizes the latter in his fervent support for the abolition of slavery and his utopian dream of individual liberty as the basis of an ordered society.[1] He was born into a New England family with its Puritan tradition of political democracy which led him to espouse the cause of unionism against the separatism of the South. His family bred poets and he naturally found his vehicle of expression in journalistic and poetical writings. In 1857 he became editor of the *Atlantic Monthly* which encouraged contributors to 'find the ideal in the real'.[2] But corruption in government led him increasingly to put his faith in the integrity of citizens. The individual, he wrote, must be 'sole sponsor of himself'. Only 'self mastery'[3] would combat the corruption of political power. These beliefs were based on a humanitarian faith, though he thought that a modern scientific outlook could be reconciled with a 'modified religious faith'.

His poetry was the eloquent expression of these ideals. *Three Memorial Odes*, envisaging true liberty as self-control grounded on a cultivated mind and tradition, brought him close to Matthew Arnold whom he greatly admired. Indeed, he had a close affinity with many English thinkers of the period. He succeeded Arnold as president of the Wordsworth Society and, from 1880 to 1885, was the US ambassador in England. Our hymn comes from a poem 'The Present Crisis', written in 1844 when the issues of slavery and separatism were reaching boiling-point. It is a trumpet-call to fight the wrong, even single-handedly if necessary. Two points stand out: first, there is a strong historical sense that God has always been present in every battle against social evil, suffering with humanity in every 'new Calvary' climbed by a bleeding Christ; and secondly, the hymn proclaims the urgent message that ancient faith must find new expressions for new occasions: the old expressions become outmoded ('uncouth'). So the idealist must be called 'upward still and onwards' to keep abreast of truth. No doubt the *NEH* dropped this hymn because of its over-optimism. Nevertheless, it surely speaks still to this age of new tyrannies, violence and martyrs.

---

[1] We thank Mrs Madeline Barber for compiling this account.

[2] *Encyclopedia Britannica, sub nom.*

[3] Ibid.

Once to every man and nation
   Comes the moment to decide,
In the strife of truth with falsehood,
   For the good or evil side;
Some great cause, God's new Messiah,
   Offering each the bloom or blight—
And the choice goes by for ever
   'Twixt that darkness and that light.

Then to side with truth is noble,
   When we share her wretched crust,
Ere her cause bring fame and profit,
   And 'tis prosperous to be just;
Then it is the brave man chooses,
   While the coward stands aside,
And the multitude make virtue
   Of the faith they had denied.

By the light of burning martyrs,
   Christ, thy bleeding feet we track,
Toiling up new Calvaries ever
   With the Cross that turns not back.
New occasions teach new duties;
   Time makes ancient good uncouth;
They must upward still and onward
   Who would keep abreast of truth.

Though the cause of evil prosper,
   Yet 'tis truth alone is strong;
Though her portion be the scaffold,
   And upon the throne be wrong—
Yet that scaffold sways the future,
   And, behind the dim unknown,
Standeth God within the shadow,
   Keeping watch above his own.

W. Walsham How (1823–97)

O nce the need to wake up parish congregations by more hymn-singing had taken hold, hymn-writing seems to have become the particular occupation of Anglican rural clergy. It was accompanied by a revolution in music-making. When Walsham How arrived at his first parish at Whittington, Shropshire, in 1851, one of the first things he did was to get rid of the existing barrel-organ and install a choir of seven boys in Eton collars. He then turned to the question of suitable hymns and hymn-books. He was one of the editors of *Church Hymns*, published by SPCK in the 1870s. In the first edition of *The English Hymnal* there were eight of his hymns. The majority of these were written for special occasions exemplifying the Anglican principle that hymns should be closely associated with the church's liturgical year. How's own description of a good hymn was '... simple, real, earnest and reverent'.[1] He certainly did not belong to the category of 'literary' hymn-writers, but he liked a rousing tune.

In 1888, How became Bishop of Wakefield, earning the nickname 'the Omnibus bishop' for his penchant for travelling by bus. He still supported the hymn industry. Ian Bradley reports an argument which turned on the question of whether tunes of doubtful musical merit should be used because they were popular. How defended the catchy three-time tune set to Ellerton's 'The day thou gavest, Lord, is ended', receiving the riposte: 'It is quite true that people like waltz tunes, but does the Bishop seriously hold that that is a reason for promoting them?'[2]

There are four hymns in our collection specifically on the theme of the saints at rest: two are medieval and feudal in their context ('Jerusalem the golden'★ and 'O what their joy'★); one is evangelical ('Give me the wings of faith'★); and now, lastly, we come to the romanticism of Victorian hymnody in 'For all the saints'. These hymns come from vastly different cultural backgrounds. How's soldier theme echoes the warrior theme of 'Jerusalem the golden', but there is a sunset glow of the Pre-Raphaelites over his triumphant host. The sweep of his words is greatly enhanced by Vaughan Williams's exultant tune.

---

[1] Bradley, *Abide with Me*, p. 199.
[2] Ibid., p. 222.

For all the saints who from their labours rest,
Who thee by faith before the world confest,
Thy name, O Jesu, be for ever blest.

Alleluya!

Thou wast their Rock, their Fortress, and their Might;
Thou, Lord, their Captain in the well-fought fight;
Thou in the darkness drear their one true Light.

O may thy soldiers, faithful, true, and bold,
Fight as the saints who nobly fought of old,
And win, with them, the victor's crown of gold.

O blest communion! fellowship divine!
We feebly struggle, they in glory shine;
Yet all are one in thee, for all are thine.

And when the strife is fierce, the warfare long,
Steals on the ear the distant triumph-song,
And hearts are brave again, and arms are strong.

The golden evening brightens in the west;
Soon, soon to faithful warriors cometh rest:
Sweet is the calm of Paradise the blest.

But lo! there breaks a yet more glorious day;
The saints triumphant rise in bright array;
The King of glory passes on his way.

From earth's wide bounds, from ocean's farthest coast,
Through gates of pearl streams in the countless host,
Singing to Father, Son, and Holy Ghost.

Christina Rossetti (1830–94)

S ister of the more famous Dante Gabriel, Christina Rossetti seems to have been overshadowed by her brother, much as Dorothy Words-worth and Fanny Mendelssohn were by theirs. Today, Christina's poetry still appears in anthologies and hymn-books while the 'vast and cloudy generalizations' of the verse of her brother are now less known than his work as a painter and as one of the founders of the Pre-Raphaelite Brotherhood.[1]

Christina's father had arrived in London in 1825 as an émigré from Italy. He encouraged his family to discuss affairs of religion, politics and culture, and Christina, who was educated at home with her older sister Maria, shared their conversation and intellectual interests. Mother and children were High Anglican in religion, followers of the Tractarian or Oxford Movement★ – as were William Morris and the Pre-Raphaelites. At twenty, Christina was engaged to the painter James Collinson, one of the original Brotherhood, but she broke off her engagement when he rejected Anglicanism to rejoin the Roman Catholic church. She never married, and, after an unsuccessful attempt to teach as a governess, she lived on the edges of the Pre-Raphaelite set in London and Kelmscott in Oxfordshire, writing poems for children, sonnets and love lyrics, and devotional works including prose and hymns.

Christina Rossetti's first poems appeared (under a pseudonym) in *The Germ*, a short-lived journal of the Brotherhood published in 1850. By 1862, many of her best-known poems, including the sinisterly erotic 'Goblin Market', were printed in various anthologies and periodicals under her own name. The strong faith of much of her religious work contrasts with a sense of unrequited love and melancholy in some of her secular poems, but there is always a sense of freshness and love of life, as in 'The Birthday', which brings together the richness of a medieval tapestry with delight in the present moment.

---

[1] *Oxford Comp. to Eng. Lit.*, p. 859.

Raise me a dais of silk and down;
Hang it with vair and purple dyes;
Carve it in doves and pomegranates,
And peacocks with a hundred eyes.
Work it in gold and silver grapes,
In leaves and silver fleurs-de-lys;
Because the birthday of my life
Is come, my love is come to me.

Alleluia Tapestry, William Morris and Edward Burne-Jones

Rossetti was an accomplished poet, technically, with a gift for creating an inner world in seemingly simple phrases. Walter de la Mare included nine of her lyrics (but only one of her brother's) in his anthology *Come Hither* of 1923, writing that her work shows a 'rhythm and poise, a serpentining of music so delicate that on clumsy lips it will vanish as rapidly as the bloom from a plum'.[1] The generations of people who have sung her best-known Christmas hymn have appreciated Rossetti's poised scene-setting and the way in which, in the last verse, she draws the singer into the original story of Christmas – a frosty view of Christmas, it is true, that owes more to the English than the Mediterranean landscape. The poem did not appear as a hymn in her lifetime but it was included in *The English Hymnal* after her death to the simple but evocative setting by Gustav Holst.

[2] Walter de la Mare, *Come Hither* (Constable, London, 1928), p. 713.

In the bleak mid-winter
    Frosty wind made moan,
Earth stood hard as iron,
    Water like a stone;
Snow had fallen, snow on snow,
    Snow on snow,
In the bleak mid-winter,
    Long ago.

Our God, heaven cannot hold him
    Nor earth sustain;
Heaven and earth shall flee away
    When he comes to reign:
In the bleak mid-winter
    A stable-place sufficed
The Lord God Almighty
    Jesus Christ.

Enough for him, whom Cherubim
    Worship night and day,
A breastful of milk,
    And a mangerful of hay;
Enough for him, whom Angels
    Fall down before,
The ox and ass and camel
    Which adore.

Angels and Archangels
    May have gathered there,
Cherubim and Seraphim
    Thonged the air—
But only his mother
    In her maiden bliss
Worshipped the Belovèd
    With a kiss.

What can I give him
    Poor as I am?
If I were a shepherd
    I would bring a lamb;
If I were a wise man
    I would do my part;
Yet what I can I give him—
    Give my heart.

Charles E. Oakley (1832–65)

Many of the Victorian hymn-writers were rural clergy who relieved their comparative isolation by this productive means – with both good and bad results. Not all were limited by narrow horizons. It is interesting to picture Charles Oakley sitting in his rectory study at Wickwar, Gloucestershire, penning his Advent hymn 'Hills of the North, rejoice', with its sweeping vision of the world and powerful rhythm. Sung to Martin Shaw's rousing tune, many of us will recall the thrill of imagination which it sparked off. Even in 1998, Libby Purves recalls this experience in her personal memoir, *Holy Smoke*, from her primary-school days:

'The best days were when - all forty-odd pupils together – we sang:

'Hills of the North, rejoice;
  River and mountain-spring,
Hark to the advent voice;
  Valley and lowland, sing!

Each verse brought new geographical excitement: 'Isles of the southern seas, deep in your coral caves ... Lands of the east awake ... Shores of the utmost west'. I was quite as romantically swayed by these notions, as if I had not already crossed half the world's oceans in great liners.'[1]

But, alas, this popular hymn is now politically incorrect: it smacks of Anglo-Saxon imperialism and had already been dropped by the first edition of *The English Hymnal*. Such a vivid hymn, however, could not be wholly discarded. The editors of the *NEH* have used it as the basis of a virtually new hymn which retains the original metre and tune. The new text loses some of the original imagery and is altogether less poetic, but it still holds the great Advent promise.

---

[1] Libby Purves, *Holy Smoke: Religion and Roots. A Personal Memoir* (Hodder & Stoughton, London, 1998), pp. 26–7. Her village school was still using the original version in the late 1950s.

Hills of the North, rejoice,
　　Echoing songs arise,
　Hail with united voice
　　Him who made earth and skies:
He comes in righteousness and love,
He brings salvation from above.

Isles of the Southern seas,
　　Sing to the listening earth,
　Carry on every breeze
　　Hope of a world's new birth:
In Christ shall all be made anew,
His word is sure, his promise true.

Lands of the East, arise,
　　He is your brightest morn,
　Greet him with joyous eyes,
　　Praise shall his path adorn:
The God whom you have longed to know
In Christ draws near, and calls you now.

Shores of the utmost West,
　　Lands of the setting sun,
　Welcome the heavenly guest
　　In whom the dawn has come:
He brings a never-ending light
Who triumphed o'er our darkest night.

Shout, as you journey on,
　　Songs be in every mouth,
　Lo, from the North they come,
　　From East and West and South:
In Jesus all shall find their rest,
In him the sons of earth be blest.

Phillips Brooks (1835–93)

I t is interesting to discover that this favourite of carol singers was written by an American bishop. Brooks was episcopal rector of Philadelphia when he pictured little Bethlehem silent beneath the stars, in 1868. How many English carol-singers subconsciously transfer that picture to a typical English village? In whatever continent we locate those silent streets of the imagination, it is the mystery of the 'wondrous gift', focused in time and place, yet bearing the 'hopes and fears of all the years', which is encapsulated here in a few simple lines of verse.

There are two English settings of this carol but the one most commonly sung is Vaughan Williams's *Forest Green*, one of the many folk-melodies which he collected and arranged for the 1906 *English Hymnal*. Another of these is an older modal melody, for G. K. Chesterton's★ 'O God of earth and altar' (NEH 492).

FOREST GREEN

O little town of Bethlehem,
How still we see thee lie!
Above thy deep and dreamless sleep
The silent stars go by.
Yet in thy dark streets shineth
The everlasting light;
The hopes and fears of all the years
Are met in thee to-night.

O morning stars, together
Proclaim the holy birth,
And praises sing to God the King,
And peace to men on earth;
For Christ is born of Mary;
And, gathered all above,
While mortals sleep, the angels keep
Their watch of wondering love.

How silently, how silently,
The wondrous gift is given!
So God imparts to human hearts
The blessings of his heaven.
No ear may hear his coming;
But in this world of sin,
Where meek souls will receive him, still
The dear Christ enters in.

Where children pure and happy
Pray to the blessèd Child,
Where misery cries out to thee,
Son of the mother mild;
Where charity stands watching
And faith holds wide the door,
The dark night wakes, the glory breaks,
And Christmas comes once more.

O holy Child of Bethlehem,
Descend to us, we pray;
Cast out our sin, and enter in,
Be born in us today.
We hear the Christmas angels
The great glad tidings tell:
O come to us, abide with us,
Our Lord Emmanuel.

John White Chadwick
(1840–1904)

A merican hymn-writers made a significant contribution to the
expression of spiritual aspirations towards a better world. It is
appropriate that John W. Chadwick should have composed his vision
of a new worldwide order for the graduating class of the Divinity School at
Cambridge, Massachusetts, in 1864. He belonged to the liberal tradition of
American thought and his hymn must surely have been an inspiration to a
generation of eager young graduates going forth to reform the world.

The hymn appeared in *The English Hymnal* to music by the distinguished
Jacobean composer, Orlando Gibbons★, Court organist for James I. Gibbons's
music had a seriousness of purpose, and, perhaps not surprisingly, the Puritan
poet George Withers (1588–1667), invited him to contribute to his collection
The Hymns and Songs of the Church, in 1623. The book, with seventeen tunes
(treble and bass) by Gibbons, was intended to be bound with Sternhold and
Hopkins, but in spite of the king's support the Stationers' Company objected
strongly and the project was dropped.

SONG I

Eternal Ruler of the ceaseless round
　　Of circling planets singing on their way;
Guide to the nations from the night profound
　　Into the glory of the perfect day;
Rule in our hearts, that we may ever be
Guided and strengthened and upheld by thee.

We are of thee, the children of thy love,
　　The brothers of thy well-belovèd Son;
Descend, O Holy Spirit, like a dove,
　　Into our hearts, that we may be as one:
As one with thee, to whom we ever tend;
As one with him, our Brother and our Friend.

We would be one in hatred of all wrong,
　　One in our love of all things sweet and fair,
One with the joy that breaketh into song,
　　One with the grief that trembleth into prayer,
One in the power that makes the children free
To follow truth, and thus to follow thee.

O clothe us with thy heavenly armour, Lord,
　　Thy trusty shield, thy sword of love divine;
Our inspiration be thy constant word;
　　We ask no victories that are not thine:
Give or withhold, let pain or pleasure be;
Enough to know that we are serving thee.

Robert Bridges (1844–1930)

Robert Bridges was born a Victorian but his most famous poem, *The Testament of Beauty*, was published in 1929 and his best-known hymn today also seems to belong to the twentieth century. He qualified and practised as a doctor but the real passion of the future Poet Laureate was for poetry. As a boy he sang sacred songs round the piano with his family; at Eton he acquired a taste for early church music; at Oxford he came under High Church influences at Pusey House. He left off practising as a doctor and moved to Yattendon Village, near Newbury, where he soon became involved, as choirmaster, in parish worship. He reinstated plainsong and sixteenth-century psalm tunes in a reaction against the worst of Victorian hymnody which he called 'maudlin' and 'washy'. He criticized modern tunes for 'plumping down on the first note of every bar whether it would or not', whereas plainsong melodies with unbarred rhythms 'dance at liberty with the voice and the sense'.[1] He finally gave up the office of choirmaster because he could not bear the vicar's sermons!

There is no denying that Bridges was a cultural élitist with antiquarian tastes. The *Yattendon Hymnal*★ was his protest against much popular church music. It was published in four parts between 1895 and 1899, on handmade paper in an archaic type-face. It only contained three tunes written after 1750: most are by sixteenth- and seventeenth-century composers such as Louis Bourgeois★, Thomas Tallis, Orlando Gibbons★ and J. S. Bach★. One might dismiss this as altogether too 'precious' for the average church worshipper. Yet the *Yattendon Hymnal* has contributed much to modern hymn collections. Thirteen of its hymns appeared in the first edition of the *English Hymnal*, translations of ancient Office Hymns and German chorales. Bridges's own translations and hymns 'speak' to the twentieth century. In later life he moved away from dogmatic Christian views but remained deeply sympathetic to Christian spirituality. In many ways he was a humanist, but one who wished to reconcile new scientific knowledge with Christian faith. This standpoint emerges not only in *The Testament of Beauty* but also in the hymn 'All my hope in God is founded', which is described as 'after Joachim Neander'. Neander (1650–81) was the headmaster of the Berlin Gymnasium and also wrote the original text of 'Praise to the Lord, the Almighty'. Although Bridges

---

[1] Bradley, *Abide with Me*, pp. 205–6.

acknowledges this source, the whole ethos of his hymn seems to belong to the twentieth century with its emphasis on a still unfolding creation. It has been described as 'stimulating theological discussion and reflection today'.[1]

All my hope on God is founded;
  He doth still my trust renew.
Me through change and chance he guideth,
  Only good and only true.
    God unknown,
    He alone
  Calls my heart to be his own.

Pride of man and earthly glory,
  Sword and crown betray his trust;
What with care and toil he buildeth,
  Tower and temple, fall to dust
    But God's power,
    Hour by hour,
  Is my temple and my tower.

God's great goodness aye endureth,
  Deep his wisdom, passing thought:
Splendour, light and life attend him,
  Beauty springeth out of naught.
    Evermore
    From his store
  New-born worlds rise and adore.

Daily doth th'Almighty giver
  Bounteous gifts on us bestow;
His desire our soul delighteth,
  Pleasure leads us where we go.
    Love doth stand
    At his hand;
  Joy doth wait on his command.

Still from man to God eternal
  Sacrifice of praise be done,
High above all praises praising
  For the gift of Christ his Son.
    Christ doth call
    One and all:
  Ye who follow shall not fall.

---

[1] Ibid., p. 237.

Henry Scott Holland (1847–1918)

Mounting Victorian concern over the social evils of contemporary society found a striking voice among middle- and upper-class hymn-writers. In our current hymn-books, working-class authors hardly appear: their songs belong rather to the mass rallies of workers' movements. Their class, however, did not detract from the passion with which men like Scott Holland wrote. He was educated at Eton and Balliol, was Precentor of St Paul's Cathedral from 1884 to 1910 and, finally, Regius Professor of Divinity at Oxford until his death. Influenced by T. R. Green, the moral philosopher, at Oxford, Scott Holland developed an independent outlook as a philosopher and theologian. In particular, he focused on relating Christian principles to the social problems of human living. With the High Churchman Charles Gore he founded the Christian Social Union in 1889, and from 1895 to 1912 he edited *The Commonwealth*, a journal devoted to such issues.

His eloquent hymn first appeared in *The Commonwealth* in 1902. It has been called 'that great Christian socialist anthem'[1] but it is not a specifically *socialist* hymn: God's judgement on the 'bitter things' in society is inescapable, but the ultimate 'solace' lies not in social planning but in feeding the hungry with 'the richness of thy word'.

---

[1] Bradley, *Abide with Me*, p. 87.

Judge eternal, throned in splendour,
   Lord of lords and King of kings,
With thy living fire of judgement
   Purge this realm of bitter things:
Solace all its wide dominion
   With the healing of thy wings.

Still the weary folk are pining
   For the hour that brings release:
And the city's crowded clangour
   Cries aloud for sin to cease;
And the homesteads and the woodlands
   Plead in silence for their peace.

Crown, O God, thine own endeavour;
   Cleave our darkness with thy sword;
Feed the faithless and the hungry
   With the richness of thy word:
Cleanse the body of this nation
   Through the glory of the Lord.

Gilbert Keith Chesterton
(1874–1936)

T he fact that hymns form a key pointer to changing social awareness is well exemplified in Chesterton's poem 'O God of earth and altar'. As we have already noted,[1] social consciences were stirring in later Victorian England. Hymns and spiritual songs were becoming instruments to rouse reformers to action. This development was partly sparked off by socialist hymns adopted from America.[2] By the turn of the century the cultural costs of industrialization were finding expression in several passionate English hymns. In 1902, Henry Scott Holland*, co-founder of the Christian Social Union, published his 'Judge eternal, throned in splendour', in the journal *The Commonwealth*. In 1906, Chesterton's verses, 'O God of earth and altar', appeared in the same publication.

Chesterton combines in a unique way a conservative theology with a romantic social vision. Two apologetic works, *Heretics* (1905) and *Orthodoxy* (1908) represent the first facet. He did, in fact, move from the Anglican to the Roman Catholic church in 1922. His social dream harks back to an idealized medieval society, suggesting the influence of Pre-Raphaelite ideas, especially William Morris's *Dream of John Ball*.[3] The hymn burns with scorn for class divisions and the power of money. Verse two forms a modern radical litany, couched in winged words. It is, however, the first two lines of the third verse that give the key to his vision: the language is deliberately archaic, striking a foreign, even a false, note today. The current individualist response to the culminating last line would be 'Who wants to be held up as a single sword?' Yet the cry 'Bind all our lives together, smite us and save us all' speaks eloquently to our atomized society.

---

[1] Above pp. 11–12.
[2] Above pp. 12–13.
[3] First printed in *The Commonwealth*, 13 November 1886 to 22 January 1887.

O God of earth and altar,
    Bow down and hear our cry,
Our earthly rulers falter,
    Our people drift and die;
The walls of gold entomb us,
    The swords of scorn divide,
Take not thy thunder from us,
    But take away our pride.

From all that terror teaches,
    From lies of tongue and pen,
From all the easy speeches
    That comfort cruel men,
From sale and profanation
    Of honour and the sword,
From sleep and from damnation,
    Deliver us, good Lord!

Tie in a living tether
    The prince and priest and thrall,
Bind all our lives together,
    Smite us and save us all;
In ire and exultation
    Aflame with faith, and free,
Lift up a living nation,
    A single sword to thee.

Eleanor Farjeon (1881–1965)

D ecades of children have probably sung 'Morning has broken' in their school assembly. Perhaps the folk-singer Cat Stevens (now Yusuf Islam), who made it a top single in the early 1970s, was one of these. Eleanor Farjeon had a literary rather than a religious background: her father was a popular novelist, her mother was the granddaughter of a famous American actor, Joseph Jefferson, and her three brothers were all involved in the arts. Although she collaborated with her brother Herbert in various theatrical ventures, Eleanor's fame rests primarily on her children's stories and verse. She wrote, she said, from inspiration, expressing herself more easily in 'running rhyme than plodding prose'.[1] She always carried pen and paper with her, and could be seen stopping on a traffic island in a busy road if a mood or impression suddenly caught her fancy.

When she was in her seventies, the children's literary world gave Eleanor Farjeon public recognition, with the prestigious Carnegie Medal for children's literature in 1955 and the first award, soon afterwards, of the American Regina Medal for her whole life's work for children.

'Morning has Broken' was especially written for the Gaelic folk melody *Bunessan*[2] at the request of Percy Dearmer, one of the editors of the 1931 edition of *Songs of Praise*. In this song of thanksgiving for a new day, Farjeon takes us in an imaginative leap right back to the very first morning in the garden of Eden before the fall, as Adam and Eve take delight in the first blackbird, the first grass, the first light. The triple dance metre and octave arpeggio-leaps of the melody are not always easy to sing, but they capture perfectly the freshness and innocence of her vision.

---

[1] Eleanor Graham, *A Puffin Quartet of Poets* (Penguin Books, London, 1958), Introduction.
[2] The little village of Bunessan is the gateway to Iona.

BUNESSAN

Morning has broken
Like the first morning,
Blackbird has spoken
  Like the first bird.
    Praise for the singing,
    Praise for the morning,
    Praise for them springing
      Fresh from the Word.

Sweet the rain's new fall
Sunlit from heaven,
Like the first dewfall
  On the first grass.
    Praise for the sweetness
    Of the wet garden,
    Sprung in completeness
      Where his feet pass.

Mine is the sunlight,
Mine is the morning
Born of the one light
  Eden saw play.
    Praise with elation,
    Praise every morning,
    God's re-creation
      Of the new day.

African-American and
Caribbean Spirituals

S ongs and spirituals are one of the great gifts of the peoples of western
Africa to the Christian church. In our hymn-books they are written
down, but they arose from an oral culture in which music was a natural
part of daily life. There were songs for digging, for gathering, for mourning
and celebrating, and, of course, for storytelling. And when, from as early as the
fifteenth century, sea captains, like John Newton★ later, kidnapped 'prime
slaves' from their African villages and shipped more than ten million across the
Atlantic in stinking and overcrowded holds, their spirit and their songs
survived that 'execrable sum of all the villainies', as John Wesley put it.[1]

Unlike tribal languages, music was an aspect of African culture which the
plantation owners did not attempt to suppress. It was therefore natural, that
during the eighteenth century, the great numbers of slaves who were
converted to Christianity should bring into their religious music a mix of
ingredients – snatches of old tunes with new words, interjections to the Lord,
responses and choruses. Often, after a rousing sermon, a listener would cry out
with a plea for forgiveness, someone else would respond, there would be a new
plea and a second answer. This is how a former slave described it to Jeanette
Robinson Murphy at the end of the nineteenth century:

> 'I'd sing [a cry to the Lord] to some ole 'shout' song I'd heard em sing from
> Africa, and dey'd all take it up and repeat it, and keep a-adding to it, and den it
> would be a spiritual.'[2]

Slaves working in the plantations or as domestic servants were able to use their
music to transcend their environment. In the guise of 'Ole Satan' the white
man could be mocked as a devil or trickster. The most persistent image in the
spirituals is that of a chosen people whom God would lead to freedom as
Moses had led his people out of Egypt. He was a personal and intimate God, as
the spirit gods of Africa had been. 'Mas' Jesus' was a bosom friend. Sister Mary
and Brother Jonah were almost part of the family. This gives a great immediacy

---

[1] J. A. Rawley, *The Transatlantic Slave Trade* (W.W. Norton & Co., New York and London, 1981),
p. 421.
[2] T. E. Fulop and A. J. Raboteau, *African-American Religions: Interpretative Essays in History and
Culture* (Routledge, New York, London, 1977), p. 64.

to African-American and Caribbean songs. 'Were you there when they crucified my Lord?' implicates all of us in the death of Christ.
Were you there when they crucified my Lord?

> Were you there when they crucified my Lord?
> Oh! Sometimes it causes me to tremble, tremble, tremble;
> Were you there when they crucified my Lord?
>
> Were you there when they nailed Him to the tree?
> Were you there when they nailed Him to the tree?
> Oh! Sometimes it causes me to tremble, tremble, tremble;
> Were you there when they nailed Him to the tree?
>
> Were you there when they laid Him in the tomb?
> Were you there when they laid Him in the tomb?
> Oh! Sometimes it causes me to tremble, tremble, tremble;
> Were you there when they laid Him in the tomb?
>
> Were you there when God raised Him from the dead?
> Were you there when God raised Him from the dead?
> Oh! Sometimes it causes me to tremble, tremble, tremble;
> Were you there when God raised Him from the dead?

'He's got the whole world in His hands', the second song, is a vast expression of faith, as God the creator cups his hands to keep his creation safe. It is often sung in the United States at public occasions. The song, from the Caribbean, describes with simplicity the story of Christmas.

Modern hymn-books give variations of both the words and musical arrangements. The syncopated rhythms of 'He's got the whole wide world' can be sung to an up-tempo jazz beat or a slow swing. *Hymns Old and New* (206) provides settings for both types of performance, and indicates where the interjections might be sung.

He's got the whole wide world in His hands,
He's got the whole wide world in His hands,
He's got the whole wide world in His hands,
He's got the whole world in His hands.

He's got everybody here, in His hands ...

He's got the tiny little baby, in His hands ...

He's got you and me brother, in His hands ...

The Virgin Mary had a baby boy,
The Virgin Mary had a baby boy,
And they said his name was Jesus.

He came from the glory,
He came from the glorious kingdom.
He came from the glory,
He came from the glorious kingdom.
O yes, believer.
O yes, believer.
He came from the glory,
He came from the glorious kingdom!

The angels sang when the baby was born, (× 3)
And proclaimed him the Saviour Jesus.

The wise men saw where the baby was born, (× 3)
And they saw that his name was Jesus.

Sydney Carter (b. 1915)

'Lord of the Dance' is one of those songs that seems always to have been there – a folk-song that was, in fact, written only in 1963 by Sydney Carter, songwriter, folk-singer and poet. The song began life on the folk-club circuit of the 1960s. Bands like The Corries gave it an Irish beat, with a backing of tin whistle and bodhram (a kind of Irish tambour, bigger than a dustbin lid), while the school choirs of Westminster and Mayfield recorded the song in a more conventional manner.[1] By 1969, 'Lord of the Dance' had arrived in the hymn-books. Today it is the fifth most popular copyright song in school assemblies (another of Carter's songs, 'One more Step', is the first). Most new hymn-books include the song, and there are any number of arrangements – from guitar or organ to a splendid full orchestral version by John Rutter.[2]

Carter's song is very much in the carol tradition, with its roots in dance rather than in church worship. He wrote in the preface to one of his song-books that his songs are 'the log book of my travelling ... I write because I like to weave a pattern and to leap about. I write, not only with my head and hand, but with my feet.'[3] In this song the Lord takes us through his own 'log book' as he tells his story in a lively, catchy rhythm, right up to the terrible events of Good Friday and Easter Day. Carter's association of dancing and religion is the more striking because dance has so often been associated with the devil[4] – hence its banning by Calvin and the Puritans. Here, in the fourth verse, Carter turns this prohibition on its head – the dance goes on, despite the devil!

The tune is adapted from a Shaker melody from the Appalachian mountains: '*Tis the gift to be simple, 'tis the gift to be free.* The American composer Aaron Copland gave the music a gentle and lyrical setting in his 1945 ballet *Appalachian Spring*.

---

[1] Donald Swann also recorded the song in the 60s (Argo EAF 48) and gave it a lively rendering in the 'Flanders and Swann' review. A member of his audience remembers vividly how he could never keep still while playing.

[2] Stainer & Bell, Catalogue no. W202 taken from their website: www.stainer.co.uk.

[3] Sydney Carter, *Songs of Sydney Carter in the Present Tense 2* (Galliard, London, 1969), Preface.

[4] The idea of Death as a dancer or fiddler in a *Danse Macabre* was common both in ancient and medieval times. Queen Elizabeth's Prayer Book of 1559 has the Dance of Death as a border throughout the Psalms. See *Oxford Comp. to Music*, p. 278.

LORD OF THE DANCE

I danced in the morning
When the world was begun,
And I danced in the moon
And the stars and the sun,
And I came down from heaven
And I danced on the earth,
At Bethlehem
I had my birth.

Dance, then, wherever you may be,
I am the Lord of the Dance, said he,
And I'll lead you all, wherever you may be,
And I'll lead you all in the Dance, said he.

I danced for the scribe
And the pharisee,
But they would not dance
And they wouldn't follow me.
I danced for the fishermen,
For James and John –
They came with me
And the Dance went on.
Chorus

I danced on the Sabbath
And I cured the lame;
The holy people
Said it was a shame.

They whipped and they stripped
And they hung me on high,
And they left me there
On a Cross to die.
Chorus

I danced on a Friday
When the sky turned black –
It's hard to dance
With the devil on your back.
They buried my body
And they thought I'd gone,
But I am the Dance,
And I still go on.
Chorus

They cut me down
And I leapt up high;
I am the life
That'll never, never die;
I'll live in you
If you'll live in me –
I am the Lord
Of the Dance, said he.
Chorus

Sebastian Temple (1928–97)

S ebastian Temple seems to have been a great seeker, and his search took him on an unconventional journey. He was born of Catholic parents in Pretoria, South Africa, an Afrikaans stronghold of the Calvinist Dutch Reformed church. By the age of 16 he had not only written a romantic novel but made enough from royalties to finance a new life in Italy. A few years later he moved to London, where the BBC employed him as an 'expert' on South African affairs. In 1958 he took off again, this time for the United States. For ten years he was a Scientologist, but when the attraction waned he finally returned to his childhood faith as a Roman Catholic. Here again he found it hard to discover his vocation. He applied to become a priest but was rejected. For the rest of his life he lived in a secular order of Franciscans, writing and composing music for use in worship.

Sebastian Temple's best-known song is 'Make me a channel of your peace', which was first published in 1967, around the time of his conversion. He based it on the prayer of self-offering attributed to St Francis:

> Lord, make me an instrument of your peace.
>   Where there is hatred let me sow love;
> where there is injury, pardon;
> where there is doubt, faith;
>   where there is despair, hope;
> where there is darkness, light.

Temple said later that he had written the song with some difficulty – that after periods of writing and prayer he eventually glanced up at the statue of St Francis and said, '"You write the bloody thing", and he did!'[1] Since publication, the song has appeared in many Catholic and Protestant hymn collections and has become a modern classic. In 1998 it reached its greatest audience when it was chosen, as a favourite of hers, to be sung at the funeral of Diana, Princess of Wales, in Westminster Abbey and was heard by millions.

---

[1] Oregon Catholic Press Publications website: www.ocp.org/composers/temple.htm

Make me a channel of your peace.
Where there is hatred, let me bring your love.
Where there is injury, your pardon, Lord,
And where there's doubt, true faith in you.

> *O Master, grant that I may never seek*
> *So much to be consoled as to console,*
> *To be understood, as to understand,*
> *To be loved, as to love with all my soul.*

Make me a channel of your peace.
Where there is hatred let me bring your hope.
Where there is darkness, only light,
And where there's sadness, ever joy.

Refrain

Make me a channel of your peace.
It is in pardoning that we are pardoned.
In giving to all men that we receive,
And in dying that we're born to eternal life.

The Iona Community

T he island of Iona off the western coast of Scotland has been a holy place at least since St Columba landed there from Ireland in 563 AD, and perhaps for longer. Celtic religious life at that time centred on the monasteries, and Iona became a focus both of learning and of Christian mission to the Scottish mainland and northern England, with daughter houses that included Holy Island of Lindisfarne on the east coast of Northumbria. Iona became a place of pilgrimage as Christians came to venerate the bones of its founder saint. It was, however, raided and sacked by Norsemen on their marauding trips around the British Isles. In 806, after one such invasion, the monks moved across to Kells in County Meath, Ireland, and it was there that the magnificent illuminated *Book of Kells* (see *St Patrick's Breastplate★*) was produced. The monastery was revived as a Christian centre around 1203, with a new Benedictine monastery and a house for nuns. The island remained an important Christian focus until 1561 when the monastic buildings were dismantled and the holy relics and most of the Celtic crosses were thrown into the sea, by order of the Protestant Convention of Estates in Edinburgh.

It was not until 1938 that Iona again began to serve as a centre for mission and spirituality when George MacLeod, a minister in the Church of Scotland, founded the Iona Community and began rebuilding the Benedictine abbey. Today the Community works on two levels. It is a place where ministers and lay Christians can withdraw to live a communal life in preparation for the demanding work ahead of them. It is also a spiritual centre for the many Christians who wish to take time out from their secular or religious environment to deepen their experience of faith and spiritual awareness. In this way Iona combines a life of political activity with spiritual healing and personal devotion. The Community remains committed to:

'Rebuilding the common life, through working for social and political change, striving for the renewal of the church with an ecumenical emphasis, and exploring new more inclusive approaches to worship, all based on an integrated understanding of spirituality.'[1]

---

[1] The Iona Community website: ionacomm@gla.iona.org.uk

The hymn given here was written by members of the Iona Community, John Bell and Graham Maule. It has been sung to the tune *Ye banks and braes*, though a different tune is given in *Mission Praise* (1990). The song combines a relevance to the problems and difficulties of modern living at its most painful with a strong sense of the divine spirit at work in our lives today.

We cannot measure how you heal
Or answer every sufferer's prayer,
Yet we believe your grace responds
Where faith and doubt unite to care.
Your hands, though bloodied on the cross,
Survive to hold and heal and warn,
To carry all through death to life
And cradle children yet unborn.

The pain that will not go away,
The guilt that clings from things long past,
The fear of what the future holds
Are present as if meant to last.
But present too is love which tends
The hurt we never hoped to find,
The private agonies inside,
The memories that haunt the mind.

So some have come who need your help,
and some have come to make amends:
Your hands which shaped and saved the world
Are present in the touch of friends.
Lord, let your Spirit meet us here
To mend the body, mind and soul,
To disentangle peace from pain
And make your broken people whole.

The Taizé Community

U nlike Iona with its long monastic tradition, a religious community in Taizé, Burgundy, has only been established for about 60 years. It was the vision of Brother Roger, in 1940, when he saw a need for reconciliation in a France divided by war, collaboration and resistance. He brought together a small Community of brothers. At first they worshipped in the local parish church, but so many visitors came to share his vision that, by the 1960s, a new church was needed: the Church of Reconciliation. The Community now numbers about 100 brothers: Roman Catholics and from different Protestant backgrounds. Every summer, in an ever-expanding building, they welcome many thousands of young people from all over the world – the Americas, the Antipodes, Africa and the Far East – to join them in Taizé's communal life and worship. Every December the community hosts a vast meeting in a different European city, while in parishes, colleges, family and youth groups of many countries there are services based on Taizé worship: Bible readings, silence, prayer and repetitive songs.

The songs created in Taizé are simple but profound. They are a key element in the worship. 'For many Christians down through the ages,' writes Brother Roger, 'a few words repeated endlessly have been a road to contemplation. When these words are sung, then perhaps they have even more of an impact on the whole personality, penetrating its very depths.'[1] A student visitor to Taizé in 1997 – Robert Stanier – puts it like this: 'They are sung over and over, creating a breathtakingly prayerful atmosphere. The attachment of simple statements of faith to simple but beautiful melodies is immensely powerful and also enables people from all over the globe to worship together as they are either in Latin, or with versions in several different languages.'[2] At Taizé, as he says, the emphasis is on the individual's relationship with God and on being loved, accepted and forgiven. There is no judgement, no prescriptive behaviour. Perhaps this is why Taizé worship has struck such a chord with many young people alienated by 'conventional' Christianity. In the modern age most people do not normally have the time, or the opportunity, to experience the contemplative life. Taizé opens up such an experience.

---

[1] Taizé website: www.taize.fr
[2] Robert Stanier, *Living in the Community* (Koinonia, Oxford, 1997) p. 30.

David J. Evans (b. 1957)

The final song in this collection, 'Be still, for the presence of the Lord', has been described as a modern classic. It is included in many mainstream hymn-books, including *Mission Praise* and *Hymns Old and New*, appears regularly in the BBC's *Songs of Praise* programme and is commonly licensed to churches and schools who use overhead projection or who compile their own service sheets. At the time of writing (February 2000) the song was voted the most popular of all the copyright hymns handled by CCL (see Introduction, p. 16).

While 'We cannot measure how you heal', from Iona*, represents the continuing Christian concern for social justice, 'Be still' takes us on an inner journey, to a place of awe and mystery where a transcendent God reveals his

DAVID J. EVANS
© 1986 KINGSWAY MUSIC

---

[1] E-mail to the authors.

presence in our mundane and ordinary lives. In the last verse the stillness is dynamic, as God's power moves within to cleanse and heal. The song has found a particular niche in places of retreat and worship as well as in regular church services where it has resonances for people from very difference backgrounds.

In the seventies, David Evans, a musician and teacher, was involved in the early house church/charismatic movement but he began to feel that it was in danger of trivializing God. 'Like Jacob at Bethel (Genesis 28),' he writes, 'I felt that we were asleep on holy ground ... I felt that our contemporary worship had been largely oblivious to the awesomeness of God's presence within it.' He wrote the song in 1985 in response to this feeling, and says now, 'I still find it rather an ordinary lyric and simple tune – but somehow the whole is greater than the sum of its parts.'[1]

> Be still,
> for the presence of the Lord,
>   the Holy One, is here;
> come bow before Him now
> with reverence and fear:
> in Him no sin is found –
> we stnad on holy ground.
> Be still,
> for the presence of the Lord,
>   the Holy One, is here.
>
> Be still,
> for the glory of the Lord
>   is shining all around;
> He burns with holy fire,
> with splendour He is crowned:
> how awesome is the sight –
> our radiant King of light!
> Be still,
> for the glory of the Lord
>   is shining all around.
>
> Be still,
> for the power of the Lord
>   is moving in this place:
> He comes to cleanse and heal,
> to minister His grace –
> no work too hard for Him.
> In faith receive from Him.
> Be still,
> for the power of the Lord
>   is moving in this place.

Copyright Acknowledgements

Copyright Acknowledgements

Index

Index of first lines

Index of first lines